Henry Cecil was the pseudony Leon. He was born in Norwood Green Rectory, near London, England in 1902. He studied at Cambridge where he edited an undergraduate magazine and wrote a Footlights May Week production. Called to the bar in 1923, he served with the British Army during the Second World War. While in the Middle East with his battalion he used to entertain the troops with a serial story each evening. This formed the basis of his first book, *Full Circle*. He was appointed a County Court Judge in 1949 and held that position until 1967. The law and the circumstances which surround it were the source of his many novels, plays, and short stories. His books are works of great comic genius with unpredictable twists of plot which highlight the often absurd workings of the English legal system. He died in 1976.

BROTHERS
IN LAW

by

Henry Cecil

HOUSE OF
STRATUS

This edition published in 2000 by House of Stratus, an imprint of
House of Stratus Ltd, Thirsk Industrial Park, York Road, Thirsk,
North Yorkshire, YO7 3BX, UK.
Also at: House of Stratus Inc., 2 Neptune Road, Poughkeepsie, NY 12601, USA.

www.houseofstratus.com

Typeset, printed and bound by House of Stratus.

A catalogue record for this book is available from the British Library
and the Library of Congress.

ISBN 1-84232-046-7

Contents

CHAPTER ONE

Call to the Bar

'George Smith is acquitted by the jury at Assizes of a criminal offence. "You are discharged," the judge says to him, and then adds: "You were very lucky in your jury." Mr Smith issues a writ against the judge claiming damages for slander. What are the first steps likely to be taken in Mr Smith's action after the service of the writ?'

Roger Thursby looked round the hall where he was about to answer this last question in his Bar Final Examination. He was fairly well satisfied with his answers to the other questions and he had done most of them quickly. So he had plenty of time for the last. He looked at the pictures of past eminent judges on the walls. Surely, he thought, no judge would behave like the one in the question. He saw sternness in some of the faces, but no trace of the meanness which seemed to him implicit in the remark made by the judge to the prisoner. The jury had acquitted the man. Presumed innocent even before the verdict, he could not be thought less so after he had been found Not Guilty. Yet, after his acquittal, the judge, merely to gratify his own personal feelings, had strongly suggested that he was guilty. And the prisoner could not hit back. Or could

1

he? That was the question. Well, there was plenty of time to answer it. How nice it was to be at the end of all his examinations; Roger was not an over-confident young man, but he knew that he had done well enough to pass at any rate. And soon he would be a barrister. Only twenty-one and a barrister. It was a great thought. There were not many young men who could be called to the Bar today at the age of twenty-one. A distant cousin of his had been called on his twenty-first birthday. But that was long before the days of military service. Roger had had to do a lot of work, and to give up quite a good deal, to be called before he was twenty-two. But he'd done it in the end. He had eaten all his dinners and had been pleased that this curious and pleasant custom was still retained as an essential qualification for admission to the English Bar. It must have been nicer still in the old days, he thought, when association in the Inns of Court with men of law and dinners with them in the evening took the place of examinations. He had enjoyed the dinners, meeting all sorts of different young men and women in the process. He had liked the sometimes quaint procedure and had been rather proud to drink a toast from a loving cup to the 'pious, glorious and immortal memory of Good Queen Bess'. And he had passed all his examinations, except this last, the Final. And now that was over, all but the last question. Well, the answer was simple enough.

'The judge,' he wrote, 'would, by the Treasury Solicitor, enter an appearance to the writ, possibly under protest, and would then apply to stay or dismiss the proceedings as an abuse of the process of the Court.' He paused and thought for a moment. Would it be too dangerous? Well, it wouldn't be fair to plough him for it. Here goes. And he wrote: 'Although I think the judge's application would be successful, as anything said by a judge in Court, however unfair or ill-advised, must be absolutely privileged if it in any way relates to the proceedings, all the same I think that the words "abuse of the process of the Court" should have stuck in that judge's throat.'

'I do hereby call you to the Bar and do publish you barrister.' The Treasurer of Roger's Inn had said the magic words and shaken hands with him, and Roger was a barrister. His optimism during the Final had been justified. Indeed, he had been placed in the first class, which he had not expected. And now here he was standing with the other newly called young men and women. The actual ceremony was finished and the Treasurer was about to deliver a short homily to them before they sat down to dinner, the first dinner he would eat in his Inn as a barrister. Possibly one day he would be doing what the Treasurer was doing. He'd better listen to what he was going to say.

'Some years ago,' began the Treasurer, 'more than I now like to think, I was called to the Bar by a most learned Master of the Bench of this Honourable Society. He spoke to us as I am now speaking to you. What he said was excellent, but I am bound to admit that there can be too much of an excellent thing – even, for example, of the admirable sherry with which this Honourable Society still provides us. Now I am not suggesting for one moment that the length of the address and the sherry had anything to do with one another – but the fact remains that he kept us standing – and waiting for our dinner – as you are now, for the best part of half an hour. Whether it was due to this I know not, but the custom of making this address thereafter fell into desuetude and has only just been revived. This brings me at once to the quality which I strongly commend to you as the second most important quality to be cultivated by you in your career. I will deal with the first in a moment. The second is brevity. Don't confuse quantity with quality. Say little and say it well. One might think that I was giving advice to a newly appointed judge, but it is almost as important for counsel to know when to hold his tongue as for a judge. But the first quality, without which no barrister ought to succeed, is a fearless integrity. That quality needs no explanation. Fearless integrity. You will nearly always know instinctively what is the right thing to do. Do it. Finally, I commend to you the quality of good fellowship – "strive mightily but eat and drink as friends". Which seems to me to be a good note on which to end this address. I wish all of you the success you deserve; I feel sure you will have it and I hope that thought will not depress too many of you.'

And, after Grace had been said, judges, barristers and students sat down to dinner.

CHAPTER TWO

The Beginning

'For my next song,' said the baritone from abroad, 'I have chosen a German one. I shall sing it in the original language but, to help you follow it, I will first give you a fairly literal translation. "In the woods the birds sing and the other animals make their personal noises. But I sit by the disused well and weep. Where there once was up-drip now there is down-drip." '

'Drip's the word,' whispered Roger to Sally. 'Can't we slip out before he makes *his* personal noises?'

'Be quiet,' said Sally.

He had to endure that song and the next, which was called – Roger thought most reasonably – "Torment", and then he managed to persuade Sally to leave.

'It really is too bad,' he said when they were safely outside the hall. 'We're supposed to be celebrating my "call" and you have to drag me there. Anyway, we're out now. Let's *go* and celebrate. I can do with some down-drip.'

'We've missed mother,' said Sally.

'Was she going to sing too?'

'You don't imagine I'd have made you come otherwise. I told you about it.'

'I believe you did, now I come to think of it – but my mind's been so full up with my "call" that I haven't been taking in much else. Have we really missed your mother?'

'Don't sound so pleased. She hasn't a bad voice at all.'

'I'm sure it's lovely. Like you are. But, oh, Sally, I can't think of anything except that I'm a barrister, a real live one. I've been one for twenty-four hours. I could defend you for murder or shoplifting. I could get you a divorce or appear at your inquest. Am I being very silly? Anyway,' he went on, without giving Sally a chance to answer, 'I haven't talked about it all the time. I did ask you to marry me, didn't I?'

'In a sort of way, I suppose – in the intervals.'

'Why did you say "no"?'

'It wasn't a definite "no".'

'It wasn't a definite "yes".'

'I suppose you'll be wanting everything "yes" or "no" now. You lawyers! Let me tell you one thing. You'll have to keep your law for the Courts. I'm not just going to be black or white. I'll be grey when I please.'

'I love you in grey. What'll you wear when you come to hear my first case?'

'First catch your fish,' said Sally. 'Besides,' she added, 'you said you'd thought of asking Joyce to marry you.'

'That was an alternative. Not both at the same time.'

'Look,' said Sally. 'You keep your beautiful legal mind for your unfortunate clients – if you get any.'

'I'm sorry, Sally. I didn't mean to be flippant – at least – I did. I am sorry, Sally. I don't know what to say. D'you think I'll ever grow up?'

'Well, twenty-one isn't all that old. Come on, cheer up. Now we *will* go and celebrate. I didn't mean to be beastly.'

A few minutes later they were drinking.

'Here's to Roger Thursby, barrister-at-law.'

'Here's to Roger Thursby, Esquire, QC.'

'Here's to Mr Justice Thursby.'

'Here's to us.'

When they parted later that evening Roger was very, very happy, though he was still uncertain whether it should be Sally or Joy. But he forgot them both when he went to sleep and all his dreams were of judges and barristers, beautiful clients and criminals. Sometimes they got a bit mixed up, but, even if they had not, they would not have borne much resemblance to the real thing.

The next day he kept an appointment at No.1 Temple Court, the chambers of Mr Kendall Grimes, a junior of many years' standing with a substantial practice, to whom he had been given an introduction. His appointment was for 9.30 and he arrived ten minutes early and introduced himself to Mr Grimes' clerk, Alec Blake.

'Good morning, sir,' said Alec pleasantly. 'I'm glad you've come early. Gives me a chance to put you in the picture. Don't suppose you know anything about the Temple, sir?'

'I don't,' said Roger. 'Not a thing.'

'Well, there's lots to learn, sir.'

He might have added, as Roger soon appreciated, that the first thing to learn on going into chambers in the Temple is the importance of the clerk.

'One thing, if I may say at once, sir,' went on Alec, 'is always to be on the spot. Stay in chambers late. Come early. You never know what may happen.'

As he made this last remark Alec sucked his teeth, and gave Roger a knowing look. It was not that there was anything in his teeth to suck, but it was a method, not entirely unknown in the Temple, of indicating that the sucker knew a thing or two. Roger shivered slightly. It was to him as cleaning windows is to some people and much as he came to like Alec he could never reconcile himself to this particular sound. On this, his introduction to it, he was too thrilled at his first contact with chambers in the Temple to be as affected by it as he became later. At that moment the telephone rang.

'Excuse me, sir,' said Alec as he answered it. 'Hullo. Yes. Mr Grimes' clerk speaking. Oh – Albert. Look, old boy, we can't do it, really we can't. Must be thirty-three. What's that? Yes, of course, I know they've a leader. I'm only asking for the junior's fee. I ought to ask for the leader's by rights. Letting you off lightly. What! Now really, old boy, it's a bit late to come that one. I dare say you don't like the two-thirds rule – but it hasn't gone yet. What's that? If we weren't on the telephone I'd tell you what you could do with that Report. No, I can't send him in for twenty-five. All right, I *won't*, if you like. Now look, old boy, what about a coffee and we'll talk it over. See you over the way? About half-eleven? OK.'

Alec turned to Roger.

'Sorry, sir. One of the things we have to do,' and he gave a loud suck. Roger tried to look as though he didn't mind the suck and had understood something of what had happened, whereas he had not the faintest idea what it was all about, and he didn't like the suck at all.

'It's most interesting,' he said. 'Is that Mr Grimes by any chance?' he went on, pointing to a photograph of someone in uniform which was hanging on the wall above Alec's table.

'It is, sir,' said Alec. 'He doesn't like my keeping it there, as a matter of fact, but I put my foot down. There were quite a number of people who stayed at home in 1914. He was in it from the start. Don't see why *I* shouldn't say so, even if *he* won't. Anyway, it's my photo and I can put it where I like. It's amazing, really, sir. You'd never think of him as a soldier. You wait and you'll see what I mean. But he went in just as a private, just as a private, sir – no pulling strings for our Mr Grimes, and how d'you think he ended up?'

'How?' asked Roger.

'As a sergeant-major, sir. If I hadn't seen him myself – I was a boy in the Temple then, sir – I wouldn't have believed it. Amazing. You'll see what I mean, sir. Mentioned twice in despatches he was, sir.'

'Jolly good,' said Roger.

The telephone rang again and just as Alec was answering it there was a noise on the staircase rather like a small express train coming up it and a second later Mr Grimes burst into the room, panting. Roger at first thought there had been an accident but he soon found out that this was Mr Grimes' normal method of entrance. Mr Grimes looked, panting, at Alec for a moment.

'It's Mr Brookes,' whispered Alec, putting his hand over the mouthpiece.

Mr Grimes nodded and then noticed Roger. He did not know whether he was a client or the prospective pupil or another barrister's clerk. So he gave him a 'Good morning' which would do for any of them and bolted into his room, which was next to the clerk's room.

Alec finished his conversation with Mr Brookes. 'Yes, sir. I'll have him there, sir. Don't you worry, sir. That's very nice of you, sir.' He turned from the telephone, obviously pleased at what Mr Brookes had said and, with one last violent suck, winked at Roger plainly indicating that there were no flies on Mr Alec Blake. Then with a: 'He'll see you in a moment, sir,' he went hurriedly into Mr Grimes' room.

Roger started to collate his first impressions of a barrister's chambers, with a view to telling Sally and Joy and his mother. It was exciting to be about to start his career, though a barrister's chambers looked very different from what he had imagined. It was not that they were clean. They weren't. Nor did he yet know that the lavatory was old-fashioned and that there was no hot water, unless you used a gas ring. He was as yet unaware that the system of cleaning was for a lady called a laundress to come in every morning, make herself a cup of tea and go on to the next set of chambers. It was just that he couldn't imagine, say, Crippen, being defended by anyone who worked in No. 1 Temple Court, which, it will be understood, was not one of the new buildings in the Temple. And Mr Grimes looked indeed very different from his idea of a busy barrister. He was tallish, thin, quite bald, except for two large tufts of coal-black hair which stood up obstinately on either side of the bald expanse and which equally obstinately refused to change their colour with the years. At the time Roger first saw him he also had bushy side whiskers which came halfway down his cheek on one side and not quite halfway down on the other. They, too, were obstinately black. Roger subsequently learned that he had once worn a drooping black moustache but that one day he had shaved it off and, like the disappointed witch in the fairy tale, it was never seen again.

There were other things, too, which Roger had yet to learn about Mr Grimes – that he was unmarried and lived near the Essex marshes with an old and feeble housekeeper who looked after him when he was not looking after her, that he kept bees, to which he was devoted, that his work, his bees, and his housekeeper appeared to be his only interests in life, that every morning he sat meekly in the driving-seat of a very fast car and drove it anything but meekly to the Temple, and that, on reaching the Temple, he jumped out as though his life depended on it and rushed to his chambers, with the result which Roger had just witnessed. His sight appeared to be extremely good, and it was said that the large horn-rimmed glasses which he wore in Court contained plain glass and were used by him simply because he found them useful for taking off when cross-examining a witness. Roger never discovered whether this rumour was based on fact or not, but he was quite satisfied that the story that Mr Grimes once appeared before the judge in chambers with each tuft of hair full of bees was entirely apocryphal.

Roger was still wondering at what he had just heard from Alec and seen in Mr Grimes when Alec came out and conducted him into Mr Grimes' room.

'This is Mr Thursby, sir.'

Mr Grimes held out his hand. 'How are ye, my dear fellow?' he said. 'How are ye?' He had a rather high-pitched sing-song way of speaking. 'So ye've come to the Bar, have ye? That's the way. Have a chair, my dear fellow. That's right, that's right.'

'Mr Milroy said you might have a vacancy for a pupil,' said Roger. 'Do you think you might be able to take me?'

'Do I think we might be able to take ye, my dear fellow? Well, my dear fellow, we might, you know, we might. Have ye been called?'

'Yes.'

'Who proposed ye?'

'Well, my mother knows Mr Milroy. He's a Bencher of my Inn, and he introduced me to Mr Sanderson.'

'When were ye called, my dear fellow?'

'The day before yesterday, as a matter of fact.'

'Just out of the egg, my dear fellow, just out of the egg. D'ye think ye're going to like it?'

'I'm sure I shall, but, of course, I don't really know much about it yet. I suppose the more important question really is whether it will like me.'

'Quite right, my dear fellow, quite right. Yes, I think we can take ye, I think we can take ye. When would ye like to start?'

'Straight away, if I may.'

'Of course ye may, my dear fellow, of course ye may. Take these papers and have a look at them. Alec will show ye where the pupils' room is. Ye'll find a couple of others there. They'll tell ye how the wheels go round. Now, off ye go, my dear fellow. Ask me anything you want to. Goodbye, my dear fellow – goodbye, bye, bye.' And Mr Grimes showed Roger to the door.

'All right, sir?' said Alec.

'Mr Grimes said I could start at once,' said Roger.

'Very well, sir. That's the pupils' room over there. I'll show you in. I hope you'll be happy here, sir.'

They started to go together towards the pupils' room door when Alec stopped for a moment.

'Oh, sir, would you make out two cheques, please. One for a hundred guineas for Mr Grimes and one for me for ten.'

'Now?'

'No – any time, sir, thank you.'

At that moment, Alec was sent for hurriedly by Mr Grimes. 'Would you mind showing yourself in, sir?' said Alec to Roger. 'I'm so sorry, sir,' and Alec rushed away.

Roger opened the door of the pupils' room and walked in. 'My name's Thursby,' he said. 'I'm a new pupil.'

'How are ye, my dear fellow, how are ye?' said a man of about thirty-three, giving a very creditable imitation of Mr Grimes.

CHAPTER THREE

First Day in Court

There were two others in the room.

'Let me introduce everyone,' said the speaker in his normal voice. 'I'm Henry Blagrove. I live here. Professionally, you know. Expect you saw my name on the door. Been there seven years. Tell you more about myself later. You'll learn about me, if nothing else, while you're here. This is Peter Hallfield. He's been a pupil six whole months. A confident young man. Though, between you and me, I can't think why. And this is Charles Hepplewhite. He's just finishing. Another month, isn't it?'

'How d'you do?' said Roger generally. 'What do I do next, please?'

'Ye'll soon learn, my dear fellow, ye'll soon learn,' said Henry. 'It's up to these chaps to say where you're to sit. Nothing to do with me. I just come in here and waste your time when I've nothing to do of my own. Which, I may tell you in confidence, is pretty often.'

'Would this do?' said Charles, indicating part of a table in the middle of the room. 'Here's a chair.'

'Thank you very much,' said Roger. He sat down and put on the table the papers which Mr Grimes had given him. On the outside was written: 'Pennythwaite v The Drum Bottling Co. (1948) Ltd. Instructions to Counsel to advise.

3 guas. Leatherhead, Frank and Compton, 4 Cockburn Buildings, EC4. Plaintiff's Solicitors.'

.. Henry looked over Roger's shoulder at the brief.

'Oh, that,' he said. 'You'll have some fun with that when you can understand it. Which is more than the Court of Appeal could. It's been twice to them and once to the House of Lords. All on a point of pleading. Now we're back where we started. Fortunately the Plaintiff's got legal aid and the Defendants are in liquidation. I don't suppose you understand what I'm talking about.'

'Quite frankly,' said Roger, 'since I arrived here I haven't understood a thing.'

'Then you've got a chance,' said Henry. 'It's people like Peter here who come to grief because they don't know a thing either but they think they do. I've done my best for him. Still do, as you can see, but it's a losing battle.'

'Henry,' said Peter, 'just because you're the most hopeless failure at the Bar and ought to have left it years ago, there's no need to be persistently offensive. He doesn't mean it, by the way,' he added to Roger. 'He just says things because he likes the sound of them. Does the same in Court. It amuses the judges, but they usually decide against him.'

'Too true,' said Henry. 'They ought to keep someone like me in every set of chambers as an awful warning.'

'Of what?' asked Roger.

'Of the result of talking too much and working too little.'

Roger soon learned all about Henry Blagrove, and one of the first things he found out was that Henry knew himself as well as any man can; that he knew, for example, that he could have succeeded at the Bar but probably never would. He was right in saying that he worked too little. He was incredibly lazy and, though sometimes he

14

would do a great deal of work in one particular case, he would avoid hard work whenever possible. He loved the life and fortunately, or unfortunately, he had just enough work to enable him to stay at the Bar. He had a keen sense of humour and fun, he was highly intelligent, cheerful and generous, but he had no inclination for the sustained hard work which he knew was necessary to success. He had very keen perception and his judgment was excellent. He had very nearly a woman's intuition and knew almost at once which way a judge's mind was working – which occasionally was more than the judge did himself. He was indeed a tremendous asset to those of Mr Grimes' pupils who were sensible enough to listen to him. He had learned very quickly the secrets of success at the Bar; he had learned the tricks of the trade; he knew the ethics; he was popular with his fellow barristers, he never broke the rules. And he was a first-class mimic, though from force of habit he was inclined to imitate Mr Grimes too often. Working so close to him he found it difficult not to do so, and was far too lazy to resist the temptation. Roger did not, of course, learn all Henry's qualities at this first meeting, but one thing he found out very quickly. Henry loved to talk.

'What would you like to know to begin with?' he asked Roger, shortly after their introduction.

'There's so much. I don't know where to begin.'

'It really is rather extraordinary,' said Henry, 'that here you are, a fully-fledged barrister, licensed to lose anyone's case for him and you haven't had an hour of practical experience. Now a medical student has to watch a lot of butchery before he qualifies to dig for his first appendix. Yet your kind old Uncle George could send you a brief tomorrow. By the way, have you an Uncle George?'

'I'm afraid not. I don't think I know any solicitors.'

'Well, it doesn't really matter, because the ones you know are seldom much use. Whenever you meet a solicitor and he learns you're at the Bar, he'll murmur something about all his work being conveyancing or litigation not much coming his way. Still, at your present stage it's just as well. When you go into Court for the first time you'll have a nice white wig and a little theoretical knowledge, but, for the rest, you'll be supported by the love of your parents and the admiration of your girlfriends. Which last, no doubt, you will do a good deal to cultivate, telling them the most thrilling stories of what you said to the judge and the judge said to you. You don't mind me lecturing like this, I suppose?'

'I'm most grateful.'

'I wish you'd shut up for a moment,' said Charles. 'I strongly suspect I'm going to be left in front of Nettlefold and I've hardly looked at the thing.'

Before Roger could begin to understand the meaning of this remark, he heard similar noises to those which he had heard when Mr Grimes had entered chambers.

'Heigh-ho,' said Charles. 'We're off.'

The next moment the door opened and Alec rushed in. Without a word he picked up the papers in front of Charles and rushed off again saying, as he went out: 'Court six first and then the Official Referee.'

'Come on,' said Charles, 'we're in this procession. You'd better make up your mind from the beginning what position you'll take up. Grimeyboy will run all the way with Alec trotting behind him. Peter, when he comes, usually goes a short head behind Alec. I walk. What'll you do?'

'Which would you advise?' said Roger to Henry. But before he could answer, Mr Grimes rushed past – while talking they had gone into the clerk's room – put a hand

16

on Roger and said: 'Come on, my dear fellow, come on. Now ye'll see what it's all about.' And down the stairs he rushed, pursued by Alec and the pupils. On this occasion Roger felt he had better keep up with his master. He caught up with him just before he crossed the Strand.

'Should I wear my robes, d'you think?' he asked.

'Oh – yes, my dear fellow. Always wear your robes. That's the way to get known. Have ye got them with ye?'

'I've left them in chambers, I'm afraid.'

'Go back for them, my dear fellow. Ye've plenty of time,' said Mr Grimes as he rushed across the Strand with Alec hard on his heels.

Roger went hastily back to chambers to collect the bag containing his robes. It was a sack-like affair of royal blue cloth with his initials embroidered on it in white and it contained a wig in a box with 'Roger Thursby Esq' painted on the lid in gold letters, three pairs of white bands and a gown. When he had ordered them he had thought that he would prefer a red to a blue bag. The assistant had coughed deferentially.

'I'm afraid that will come a little later, sir,' he had said. 'You start with a blue one.'

'What are the red ones for?'

'Well, sir, in a sort of way you get presented with a red bag, though it'll cost you a guinea.'

'What do you mean?'

'Well, a leader, sir, a QC, will give you one for doing well in a case in which he leads you. Then you give his clerk a guinea. I've never been able to think why. He doesn't pay for the bag. I hope you'll get one all right, sir.'

'Supposing I don't?'

The assistant had coughed. 'Well, sir,' he had said, 'there are people who never get a red bag, but between you and

17

me, sir, if you don't get one in your first seven years, you won't have made much headway.'

Roger found his robes and hurried across to the robing room. Mr Grimes had already gone, but he found Henry there.

'It's easy to get lost,' he said. 'I thought I'd come and guide you. It's a bit hectic this morning.'

'That's awfully kind of you,' said Roger and robed himself as quickly as he could. 'Have you any idea what I'm going to hear?' he asked.

'Well, I believe the thing before Nettlefold is a running down case and then there's a building reference before the Official Referee. Normally you'll at least be able to look at the briefs before you go into Court.'

Henry led Roger to Queen's Bench Court 6, where they were just in time to see the judge arrive. Then Henry returned to chambers.

'Fisher against Mollet,' called the associate, the bewigged official sitting below the judge, and Mr Grimes at once got up.

'May it please your Ludship,' he began. He was one of the few counsel who still used that pronunciation of Lordship. 'I appear in this case for the plaintiff with my learned friend Mr Hepplewhite. My learned friend Mr Ferret appears for the defendant. Me Lud, this is a claim for damages for personal injuries.'

'A running down case, is it, Mr Grimes?' asked the judge.

'Yes, me Lud, on the Watford by-pass. My client was driving very slowly along the main road when the defendant suddenly came out of a side turning with no warning at all and there was a collision.'

'Why was your client going at such a slow speed? It is unusual on that road, to say the least of it.'

'Oh, me Lud, he was in no particular hurry and, if I may say so, driving most carefully.'

'So you say, Mr Grimes. But if he was going so slowly, one wonders why he couldn't stop before the collision. But I suppose we'd better wait until it comes out in the evidence. Is the special damage agreed?'

'Yes, me Lud, except for one item.'

'What is the agreed amount?'

'One hundred and twenty-five pounds, me Lud. That is for repairs to the car and loss of wages.'

'What is the item not agreed?'

'A pair of trousers, me Lud. I can't think why my learned friend won't admit it.'

'Let me see,' said the judge. 'You're claiming £7 10s. They were new, I suppose?'

'Oh, yes, me Lud.'

'You want to fight the pair of trousers, do you, Mr Ferret?' asked the judge.

'Well, my Lord, no bill has been produced nor have the trousers.'

'Well, I hope we're not going to spend too much time on them,' said the judge. 'If we do, one side or the other would be able to buy a whole suit with the amount expended in costs.'

'Oh, me Lud, I shall be very short about them. But if my learned friend wants me to prove the trousers, I'll have to prove them. I don't see why my client should make him a present of them.'

'I gather they wouldn't be much use now, Mr Grimes. Now, don't let's waste any more time. Is there a plan?'

'Yes, me Lud.'

'Thank you. Is there an agreed medical report?'

'Yes, me Lud.'

'Thank you. Very well – perhaps you'll call your first witness. I'll read the report in due course.'

So began the first accident case which Roger had ever seen tried. After the second witness had been called, Roger noticed Alec hovering close to the row in which Mr Grimes and he were sitting. Suddenly, Mr Grimes whispered to him.

'Come and sit this side of me, my dear fellow.'

Roger did as he was told. This brought Mr Grimes nearer to the end of the row. A moment later he had exchanged seats with Charles who now sat next to Roger. A moment later Mr Grimes was gone. There was a slight sound from the breeze caused by his gown as he rushed away through the door of the Court, followed by Alec.

'Ought I to follow him?' whispered Roger to Charles.

'Do what you something well like, my dear chap,' said Charles with unexpected asperity. 'I'm left with this ruddy thing and I haven't read half of it.'

'Yes, Mr, Mr – er, Hepplewhite,' said the judge, 'do you wish to re-examine?'

Charles got to his feet and cleared his throat – a sure sign in an advocate of nervousness, varying from the slight to the verge-of-tears variety. In Charles' case it was between the two. He no longer wanted to cry, only to run away. It is indeed somewhat of an ordeal for a young man in his first year at the Bar to be left with a case in the High Court. The fact that he has only looked at the brief and does not know it thoroughly does not make very much difference to the way he conducts it, but it certainly does not increase his self-confidence.

'If you please, my Lord.' He cleared his throat again and began: 'My learned friend has asked you whether you hooted. Are you quite sure that you did?'

Mr Ferret immediately got up, looked sorrowfully at Charles, said to the judge: 'Really, my Lord!' and sat down.

Roger, who had a vivid imagination, wondered what on earth he himself would do. Obviously the judge and Mr Ferret knew what was happening though the glances they exchanged conveyed nothing to Roger. He felt very sorry for Charles and hoped that he'd never find himself in the same position. The judge looked in a kindly manner at the white wig of Charles and said: 'Mr Ferret thinks that was rather a leading question, Mr Hepplewhite. I'm afraid I'm inclined to agree.'

A leading question, of course, thought Roger. But what on earth does one ask instead? Would 'Did you hoot?' be a leading question. Perhaps it would be better to say, 'Did you or did you not hoot?' A moment later Roger experienced a thrill of pleasure.

'Did you or did you not hoot?' asked Charles.

'He has already said that he's not really sure,' said the judge. 'Can you carry it much further than that?'

'If your Lordship pleases,' said Charles and sat down.

'Don't you want to ask him anything about the trousers, Mr Hepplewhite?'

'The trousers, my Lord?' said Charles unhappily. The judge appeared to have made it plain at the outset that he did not want to hear too much about the trousers. And now here he was inviting him to go into the matter. The fact was that the plaintiff had been somewhat knocked about in cross-examination over the trousers. The judge was not sure that he had done himself justice in his answers to Mr Ferret. The witness was a nervous young man and had been rather over-persuaded to agree to things to which the judge was not at all satisfied he intended to agree. A few well-directed questions in re-examination might have restored the position. But Charles was quite incapable of asking them.

'The trousers, my Lord?' he said again.

What on earth would I ask? thought Roger. This is a pretty nerve-wracking game. I wonder if I ought to have gone on the Stock Exchange.

Seeing that Charles was quite incapable of dealing with the matter, the judge himself proceeded to ask the necessary questions and a few others too, some of them leading. Mr Ferret grimaced. He couldn't stop the judge asking leading questions and he saw what was going to happen. Until Mr Grimes returned, the judge was in effect going to conduct the case on behalf of the plaintiff and by the time Mr Grimes did return, he would have got so used to it that he might have become unconsciously in the plaintiff's favour. Justice is a funny thing. It can never be perfect. Roger learned in due course that sometimes the poorer counsel wins a case just because he's so bad that the judge has to step in. So what seemed unfair to the one side becomes unfair to the other.

After the running down case had been going on for some little time, Roger felt someone touch his arm. It was Alec.

'Have you seen Mr Hallfield anywhere?' he asked anxiously.

'I haven't, I'm afraid,' said Roger.

'Well, would you come with me, please, sir,' said Alec. 'It's rather urgent.'

Roger went clumsily in front of Charles, brushing some of his papers to the floor in the process, got out of counsel's row and was soon trotting after Alec through what seemed like endless corridors. He wanted to ask Alec all sorts of questions but the pace was too fast. Eventually they reached a Court.

'In here, sir,' said Alec.

Mr Grimes was on his feet addressing the Official Referee.

'If your Honour pleases,' he said, 'I submit that in meal or in malt the onus of proof is on the defendant.'

'Why meal or malt, Mr Grimes?' said Sir Hugo Cramp, the Official Referee.

'If your Honour pleases,' said Mr Grimes with a deferential smile.

'Yes, but why, Mr Grimes? You're always saying in meal or in malt, and I can't think why, I really can't.'

'Just a phrase, your Honour, just a phrase.'

'Well, you've said it three times in half an hour. I made a note of it.'

Indeed, that was the only note that Sir Hugo had so far made. The stage for making notes had not yet arrived and he hoped that it never would – except for doodling and the like and making notes of Mr Grimes' stock expression. The case ought to be settled. So should all building references. And in Sir Hugo's Court they nearly always were. It was a good thing for everyone. It saved the parties expense and Sir Hugo time, and it resulted in the next litigants' cases coming on earlier for trial – or settlement.

'Take a note, my dear fellow,' whispered Mr Grimes to Roger.

'What in?' asked Roger.

'A notebook, my dear fellow – I'm sorry, your Honour. I was just arranging with my learned friend Mr – Mr Thorburn – '

'Yes, yes,' said Sir Hugo, 'but these devilling arrangements should be made beforehand. I take it that I'm going to be deprived of the pleasure of hearing your further argument, Mr Grimes.'

'Only for a very short time, your Honour. I'm on my feet before Mr Justice Nettlefold.'

Sir Hugo removed his spectacles and looked at Mr Grimes, with a puzzled air for a moment, 'Oh, of course,' he said. 'The prophetic present. Well, I mustn't keep you, Mr Grimes. Very good of you to have come at all and I'm sure your learned junior will fill your place admirably while you are away.'

'It's very good of your Honour,' said Mr Grimes and with a few whispered words to Roger – 'Ye'll be all right, my dear fellow, just tell him the tale, just tell him the tale,' Mr Grimes was gone.

It had all happened so quickly that Roger had difficulty in realizing that he, Roger Thursby Esq, barrister-at-law, aged twenty-one, called to the Bar two days previously, had been left in Court to represent one side or the other (he did not know which) in a building dispute before a judge called an Official Referee, of whom he had only vaguely heard. He looked round the Court. There was not a face he knew. Something inside his head began to go round and round and the Official Referee's face started to approach him with alarming swiftness. He realized that he must pull himself together or faint. Sir Hugo addressed him: 'Now that the wind has dropped, Mr Truefold, would you continue your learned leader's submission?' Roger wished he had fainted. He rose unsteadily, and looked blankly in front of him.

'Your learned leader was saying,' went on Sir Hugo who, without intending to be unkind, enjoyed this sort of scene immensely, 'let me see – what was he saying? Something about malt, I believe. Strange, in a building dispute. Ah – no, I remember – he was submitting that the onus was on the other side. No doubt you would like to elaborate the submission?'

Roger continued to look blankly in front of him. It was not that the power of speech had left him, but he simply did not know what to say. He had sufficient presence of mind to realize that, if he started, 'Your Honour' and then paused, the Official Referee would, after waiting a decent interval, say, 'Yes, Mr Truefold?' and then he would either have to repeat, 'Your Honour' or lapse into silence again. It was better not to break it at all unless and until he could think of one sentence which meant something. The only sentence he would think of was: 'I want to go home,' and that wouldn't do at all. It flashed through his mind that he could pretend to faint and he cursed himself for having resisted a moment before the genuine impulse to do so. But he had a natural inclination to tell the truth. This was sometimes embarrassing in his relations with Sally and Joy, but they were a long way from his mind at this particular moment. He remained standing and staring and thinking for the thoughts which would not come.

'Come, Mr Trueband,' said Sir Hugo affably, 'it's quite calm now. Shall we proceed?'

There was nothing for it. 'Your Honour,' he began – and then came the inevitable pause. Sir Hugo looked enquiringly at him, and so did counsel on the other side and, indeed, nearly everyone in the Court.

The pause had already passed the stage at which it became unbearable when Sir Hugo duly came in with the expected 'Yes, Mr Truefold?' to which Roger replied with the only words he had so far learned: 'Your Honour,' and again there was that terrible pause. Eventually Sir Hugo broke it with: 'I suppose you say that the defendants, having admitted that the work was done and that it has not been paid for, it is for them to show that parts of it have not been properly done?'

With relief which he could not conceal, Roger added a word to his repertoire. 'Yes, Your Honour,' he said, and getting bolder – 'I do.' Then, 'Your Honour,' he added, in case the emphasis sounded rude.

'An admirable submission, Mr Truelove,' said Sir Hugo, 'and very succinctly put. But,' and he paused and frowned for a moment. 'But,' he went on, 'isn't it for the plaintiff in the first instance to give evidence that he has performed his contract – and can he do that without showing that the work was properly done?'

Roger's boldness vanished. The only truthful answer he could make would have been: 'I don't know.' But that wouldn't do. So he adopted his first line of defence, of standing and staring, keeping a 'Your Honour' in reserve for use if necessary.

'You can't very well rely,' went on Sir Hugo, 'on the maxim *omnia rite*, etc – incidentally, I never can remember exactly how it goes.'

'*Omnia rite ac sollemniter esse acta praesumuntur*,' said Roger, thanking his patron saint for making him learn that legal maxim for his Bar examinations.

'Thank you, Mr Tredgold,' said Sir Hugo, 'thank you very much. But you can't rely on that maxim in a case such as the present, can you?'

At any rate, there was an answer to that which made sense.

'I suppose not, Your Honour.'

'Or *can* you, perhaps?' went on Sir Hugo. 'I'm not sure. Perhaps you could refer me to one or two of the authorities on the point.'

At this juncture, Roger's opponent could not resist getting up and saying: 'Surely, Your Honour, there is no presumption in law that a builder always does the right thing. If there were any presumption I should have thought it would have been the other way about.'

'Well, to whom does the presumption apply, do you think?' said Sir Hugo, mercifully directing his question to Roger's opponent. 'To Official Referees, perhaps?'

At that moment Alec came into Court, although Roger did not see him. Mr Grimes had managed to take over the reins from Charles in the running down case, not without a little obstruction from Mr Justice Nettlefold who disliked Mr Grimes' habit of chopping and changing and who, besides, was now running cheerfully along with the plaintiff. 'Mr Hepplewhite is deputizing very satisfactorily for you, Mr Grimes,' the judge said quite untruthfully – except in the sense that, as the judge was doing all the work for the plaintiff, it was quite satisfactory from that gentleman's point of view. However, eventually the judge allowed himself to be persuaded and Mr Grimes took over. The plaintiff did not do quite so well after that. This was no fault of Mr Grimes'. It is just the way things happen. Once Alec had seen Mr Grimes safely into Court before Mr Justice Nettlefold he returned to the Official Referee's Court to see what was happening there, ready to send the junior clerk – who had now come over with him – sprinting round to fetch Mr Grimes if disaster seemed imminent.

'Anyway,' went on Sir Hugo, 'isn't there anything to be done in this case? Is there a Scott Schedule, Mr Truebland?' and he turned pleasantly and enquiringly to Roger. Roger was still standing and the relief when the Official Referee started to address his opponent was so great that he had begun to feel the warm blood moving through his veins again. But at the mention of 'Scott Schedule' it froze again. What on earth was a Scott Schedule? He thought of Sir Walter Scott and Scott the explorer. He thought of

Scotland. Perhaps Sir Hugo had said Scotch Schedule. Just as people sometimes have an insane urge to throw themselves in front of tube trains, Roger suddenly had an urge to say: 'No, Your Honour, but I think there's an Irish stew.' That would be the end of his career at the Bar. Short and inglorious. But over. No more standing and staring and freezing and boiling. Which is worse, a cold sweat or a hot sweat? All these thoughts crammed themselves confusedly into his mind as he stood miserably waiting. Then he heard a voice from the ceiling of the Court: 'A Scott Schedule, Your Honour?' it said.

He knew that it was his voice really, but he did not feel himself speak and he never knew his voice sounded like that.

'Yes, Mr Trueglove. Is there one? Or perhaps Mr Grimes ran away with it.'

Roger endeavoured to smile, but it was very difficult. After what seemed an age his opponent came to his rescue.

'I'm afraid there isn't, Your Honour,' he said.

'And why not?' asked Sir Hugo. 'How am I expected to try this case without a Scott Schedule? How many items are there in dispute?'

'About fifty, Your Honour.'

'Fifty,' Sir Hugo almost screamed. 'This is intolerable.'

'It's the plaintiff's responsibility,' said Roger's opponent. 'He has the carriage of the proceedings.'

'I don't care whose responsibility it is,' said Sir Hugo feigning an indignation which he did not in the least feel. It was a first-class opportunity for browbeating the parties into settling the case. 'It's quite outrageous. You and your opponent had better put your heads together. I shall rise now for ten minutes and after that time I expect to be told that you and he are well on the way to a compromise. This is an expensive court, you know.' He frowned for a moment and then looked cheerfully at counsel. 'It doesn't matter to me in the least,' he went on, 'whether you settle or not. If I don't try this case, I shall try another. I'm just thinking of the parties.'

Roger looked enquiringly at his opponent, who gave him a faintly perceptible wink.

'And in any event, I'm not going to try it without a Scott Schedule. The case will have to be adjourned anyway, but I'll give you a chance to settle it first.'

Sir Hugo rose, bowed to counsel and withdrew to his room.

As soon as Alec had seen what was happening he had sent his junior at full speed to fetch Mr Grimes. Meantime, Roger's opponent, a man named Featherstone, turned to him and said: 'Well, my boy, there we are. What shall we do about it? I'll give you a hundred and fifty. Not a penny more. You'd better take it, or you'll only have the costs to pay. You know what the old boy's like about costs. No Scott Schedule, indeed,' and Mr Featherstone rubbed his hands. 'No Scott Schedule, my dear boy. What d'you think of that?' and he laughed heartily.

'Would you very much mind telling me what a Scott Schedule is, please?' asked Roger.

'Haven't the faintest idea, my dear boy. Never come to this Court if I can help it. But it's something the old boy wants. No Scott Schedule, that's bad, isn't it? Well, what about it? Will you take a hundred and fifty?'

'I think I'd better wait till Mr Grimes comes back,' said Roger.

'Wait till he comes back? We'll be here all night. He's probably on his way to the House of Lords at the moment, just giving a friendly look in to the Court of Appeal on his way. He won't be back. Not on your life. No Scott Schedule, now I ask you!'

At that moment Roger heard with a mixture of relief and distaste a sound he recognized. It was Alec giving a loud suck.

'Mr Grimes will be here in a minute. I've sent for him.'

'What'd I better do?' whispered Roger.

'Just hang on, sir,' said Alec. 'Don't agree to anything.' Alec emphasized this last remark in the usual way.

Roger turned to his opponent.

'Mr Grimes is on his way.'

'I've heard that one before. Well – I hope he won't keep us all night. P'raps he's gone to fetch the Scott Schedule. You're a pupil, I suppose?'

'Yes.'

'How d'you like it?'

'I only started today. I find it a bit hair-raising, I'm afraid.'

'You'll soon get used to it with old Grimes. I wish he'd be quick. I'd like to go and have a cup of coffee. D'you know where he is as a matter of fact?'

'He's doing an accident case before Mr Justice Nettlefold.'

'Is he, by Jove? Well – *he* won't let him go.'

At that moment in Queen's Bench Court 6 Mr Grimes became aware that his junior clerk was making urgent signs to him. He was in the middle of cross-examining a witness.

'I had no chance of avoiding the crash,' said the witness.

'So that's what ye say, is it? We shall see,' said Mr Grimes. 'We shall see.'

'I wish you wouldn't make these comments,' said the judge. 'I know they don't mean anything and that we may never see and that, as there isn't a jury, it doesn't much matter whether we do see or we don't, but cross-examination should be used for asking questions and asking questions only. You can make your comments when you address me.'

'If your Ludship pleases. So ye couldn't avoid the accident, couldn't ye?'

'No.'

'Why didn't ye put on your brakes?'

'I did.'

'Oh, ye did, did ye? Then why didn't ye stop?'

'I did.'

'Oh, ye did, did ye? Then why did the accident happen?'

'Because the plaintiff ran into me.'

'Oh, he ran into ye, did he? I suggest ye ran into him.'

'It was the other way round. The damage to the cars shows it.'

'Oh, it does, does it? We shall see,' said Mr Grimes. 'We shall see.'

'Mr Grimes,' began the judge, but he was too late. Mr Grimes was on his way out.

A minute later he came, panting, into the Official Referee's Court.

'At last,' said Featherstone.

'I'm so sorry, my dear fellow,' said Mr Grimes. 'So sorry to have kept ye. Now, what's it all about?'

'The old boy wants us to settle.'

'Oh, he does, does he? Well, that's simple enough, my dear fellow. You just pay and it's all over.'

'I'll pay you something.'

'That's very good of ye, my dear fellow, very good of ye. Ye've had all the work done and ye'll pay something! Ye wouldn't like us to build another house for ye as well?'

'Well, you'll need to, I should think. This one's falling down already.'

'Is it really, my dear fellow? Funny your clients are still living in it then.'

'Come on, let's go outside. We've got to settle it somehow. The old boy isn't going to try it.'

The upshot of it all was that eventually the defendant agreed to pay Mr Grimes' client £300 and all his costs, and there was then a rush back to the other case, where they arrived just in time to find the judge rising for lunch.

'Come on, my dear fellow,' said Mr Grimes. 'Come and get a bite while there's time. So good of ye to have helped me. Thank ye so much.' He led Roger at a fast trot to the restaurant in the crypt at the Law Courts. There Mr Grimes helped himself to a plate of meat and salad, asked for a cup of coffee and took it to a marble-topped table which was no different from any others, except that it bore a notice: 'The seats at this table, are reserved for Counsel from 12 o'clock until 2 o'clock.'

Roger felt very important sitting at such a table and even the ordinary nature of the food and the noise made by Mr Grimes in getting rid of his as fast as possible did not spoil his pleasure. Between the bites and swallows, Mr Grimes asked Roger if he thought he'd learned anything and how he liked his first morning. Before Roger could reply, he went on to criticize Queen's Bench Judges, Official Referees and his opponents in each of the cases, finally ending up his criticisms with the pronouncement: 'But there you are, my dear fellow, they will do these things, they will do these things.'

Five minutes later they were off again, this time at only a very fast walking pace. They went to a place known as the 'Bear Garden' where Mr Grimes had a summons to dispose of before a judicial officer called a Master. It was to be heard by Master Tiptree. Before they went into the Master's room, Mr Grimes was joined by Alec and the clerk from the solicitors instructing him. Mr Grimes greeted the clerk most affably and then proceeded to say something to him in a low voice. Roger could only catch that it began with: 'I don't mind telling you, my dear fellow – ' but what he didn't mind telling him, Roger never heard. Fortunately they did not have to wait long and soon they were in front of Master Tiptree. Roger knew from his Bar examinations that various applications in the course of an action were made to a Master, but he only had a slight theoretical knowledge of such matters. A Master appearing in a question in an examination paper is very different from an actual live one sitting in his room.

'This is an application for discovery of specific documents, Master,' began Mr Grimes.

'Where's the affidavit?' asked the Master.

'Oh, Master, before we come to the affidavit, I'd like to tell you something about the action.'

'I dare say you would, Mr Grimes, but I want to see the affidavit.'

'If you please, Master.'

Mr Grimes obtained a sheet of paper from the solicitor's clerk and handed it to the Master.

He glanced at it, threw it back at Mr Grimes and said: 'What d'you call that, Mr Grimes?'

Mr Grimes looked at the offending document. 'I'm so sorry, Master. It's the wrong affidavit.'

'I am only too well aware of that, Mr Grimes. I want the right one.'

'Here it is, Master. I'm so sorry.'

Mr Grimes handed another affidavit to the Master, who read it quickly.

'This won't do, Mr Grimes. It doesn't say the alleged missing document relates to the matters in question.'

'Oh, but Master, if you'll be good enough to look at the pleadings, you'll see it must be material.'

'I dare say, Mr Grimes, but Order 31, Rule 19A is quite definite and has not been complied with.'

'Oh, but Master – '

'It's no good saying, "Oh, but Master," Mr Grimes. You know as well as I do your affidavit is defective. D'you want an adjournment or shall I dismiss the summons?'

Mr Grimes' opponent then intervened.

'Master, I ask you to refuse an adjournment and dismiss the summons.'

'I dare say you do, but I'm not going to. You can have the costs thrown away.'

'But Master – '

'I've made up my mind. You can go to the judge if you don't like it. Now Mr Grimes, have you made up your mind?'

'Yes, please, Master. I ask for an adjournment to put the affidavit in order.'

'Very well.'

The Master started to write out his Order.

Mr Grimes whispered to Roger: 'Just stay and take the Order, my dear fellow,' and without another word he was off towards Mr Justice Nettlefold's Court.

The Master wrote for a few moments. When he looked up he saw that Mr Grimes had gone.

'Pupil?' he asked Roger.

'Yes, Master.'

'How long?'

'Today.'

'Order 31, Rule 19A mean anything to you?'

'Not a thing, Master.'

'I should look it up when you get back to chambers, if I were you. It's the only way to learn the practice. You can't learn it in a vacuum. But if you look up everything that happens, you'll get a reasonable knowledge of it in time.'

'Thank you very much, Master.'

'Not at all. Good luck to you.'

Roger left the Master's room with the solicitor's clerk. 'Never heard Master Tiptree so agreeable,' said the clerk. 'He threw a book at me once.'

With difficulty Roger found his way back to the Court. The judge was giving judgment in favour of Mr Grimes' client. No sooner was it over than there was a frantic dash back to chambers, where Mr Grimes had several conferences.

Charles and Roger went into the pupils' room together. Henry was there reading *The Times*.

'Where's Peter?' asked Charles.

'He went off to the Old Bailey,' said Henry. 'Said building cases weren't in his line. Gosh!' he went on. 'You don't mean to tell me Thursby got landed with it instead?'

'He did,' said Charles, 'but he's still breathing.'

'Poor fellow,' said Henry. 'Tell me about it in your own unexpurgated Billingsgate.'

Roger told him.

'Well, well, well,' said Henry. 'He wins one case and settles the other and, knowing Grimeyboy, his client won't have lost on the deal. What I say is *fiat justitia ruat Grimes*, or, as the poet says,

"*So justice be done,*
Let Grimeyboy run." '

CHAPTER FOUR

At Home

Mrs Thursby, Roger's widowed mother, was, she hoped, making a cake when Roger arrived home after his first day as a pupil.

'Darling, how nice,' she said. 'You can give it a stir. I want to go and try on a new dress. Aunt Ethel sent it me. She's only worn it once. Just keep on stirring. I'm sure it'll be all right. Anyway, we can always give it to Mrs Rhodes. Oh, no, she doesn't come any more. Let me see, who is it now – '

'Mother, darling,' said Roger, 'I've had my first day in the Temple.'

'Of course, darling, how silly of me. Did you enjoy it? I won't be a moment. Just keep on stirring.'

And Mrs Thursby went to her bedroom. She was a young forty-eight. She had lost her husband soon after Roger was born. For some reason that neither she nor Roger, after he grew up, could understand, she had never married again. She was attractive and kind and plenty of men have no objection to butterfly minds. Roger's father, who had been a man of the highest intelligence and intellectual capacity, had adored her. So did Roger.

He stirred the mixture in the pudding bowl and as he did so he went over in his mind all that had happened during the day. Now that he was safely home it gave him a considerable thrill to think he had actually spoken in Court. He must tell his mother, though she wouldn't really take in the significance. But he must tell Sally and Joy. Which first? He stopped stirring and went to the telephone. It was Joy's turn really, he supposed.

'Joy – yes, it's me. Are you free this evening? I've quite a lot to tell you. Oh – what a shame. Can't you come and have a drink first? Yes, do, that'll be lovely. Come straight over. See you in ten minutes.'

He went back to the kitchen.

'Roger,' called his mother, 'do come and look.'

He went to her bedroom.

'It's lovely, isn't it? And I did need one so badly. I can wear it for the Fotheringays. Don't you like it?'

'I do, darling. D'you know I spoke in Court today?'

'Did you really, darling? How very nice. What exactly did you say? Don't you like the way the skirt seems to come from nowhere?'

'It suits you to a T.'

'D'you really think so?'

'Of course I do. I didn't actually say very much.'

'No, of course not. They couldn't expect very much to begin with. I expect you'll say more tomorrow.'

'Joy's coming round for a drink. You don't mind?'

'Of course not. I think she's a sweet girl. It makes me look thinner, doesn't it?'

At last Joy arrived and Roger was able to tell someone all about his first day.

'I think you're wonderful,' said Joy. 'I should love to come and hear you. When can I?'

'Well, of course, I don't know exactly when I shall be speaking again.'

'Was it a murder case?'

'Well – no, as a matter of fact.'

'Breach of promise?'

'As a matter of fact, it was a building dispute.'

'It sounds terribly dull. Weren't you bored?'

The one thing Roger had not been was bored.

'You see, things which don't sound of interest to the layman are very interesting to lawyers.'

'I don't think I should terribly care to hear a building dispute. All about houses and things. Still, I suppose you have to start somewhere. Must take time to work up to a murder case.'

'Joy, dear, you don't work up to a murder case.'

'But surely, Roger, you're wrong. I've always understood you start with silly things like debt collecting and business cases, like your building dispute, I suppose, and eventually work your way into real cases like murder and blackmail and divorce and so on. Anyway, what did you say? Did you make the jury cry? It must have been very clever of you if you did with a building dispute. But then you are so clever, Roger, that I wouldn't put it past you.'

'They don't have juries with Official Referees.'

'Sounds like football.'

'Well, it isn't. An Official Referee is a judge. You call him "Your Honour". He's very important. This one was called Sir Hugo Cramp.'

'Well, what did you say to him?'

'Well, among other things – I quoted a legal maxim to him. He thanked me very much.'

'Did it win you your case?'

'Well, it wasn't exactly my case.' He paused for a moment. Then very seriously he said: 'Joy, d'you think I'll ever be any good? I was terribly frightened.'

'You frightened? I can't believe it. You're pulling my leg.'

'I'm not. Really, Joy, I'm not.'

'What's frightening about it? You just get up and say what you want and then sit down.'

'And suppose you don't know what to say?'

'Then don't get up.'

'But I had to.'

'But I don't see why. It's a free country. Anyway, next time make certain what you want to say, get up and say it and sit down.'

'You make it sound very simple.'

'Well, Uncle Alfred's a solicitor. Which reminds me – I suppose he might send you a brief one day. Would you like that, Roger?'

'Oh, Joy, it would be wonderful.'

'What would you do if I get Uncle Alfred to send you a brief?'

'What would you like me to do?'

'There's something I'd like you not to do.'

'What?'

'Not see Sally.'

'Oh,' said Roger, unhappily. 'D'you think that's quite fair?'

'It's just as you like. I'm sure Uncle Alfred has got lots of young men to send briefs to. He'll bear up.'

'But, Joy dear, it's so difficult. And it wouldn't be fair to Sally.'

'That's right, dear – always the little unselfish one, thinking of other people. You're too good for this world.'

'Who are *you* going out with, anyway?'

'A friend of mine.'

'So I gathered. Do I know him?'

'Who said it was a him?'

'I did. Who is it?'

'D'you want to know all that much?'

'Not if you don't want to tell me.'

'Then why ask me?'

'Oh, Joy – don't let's quarrel. It's my first day at the Bar. And I want you to share it with me.'

'I'd love to share it with you – but not with you and Sally.'

'I rang you before her.'

'You went out with her last night.'

'How d'you know?'

'Now I know you did. Oh, Roger, why can't we just be married and live happily ever after?'

'We're so young, Joy. We don't any of us know our minds yet. I'd marry you both if I could.'

'Thanks very much. P'raps you'd like power to add to our number. It's George Utterson as a matter of fact.'

'That oaf.'

'He's not in the least an oaf. He's going to be Prime Minister one of these days. *He's* not frightened to talk in public. I heard him at a meeting the other day. He was grand. They applauded like anything.' She stopped for a moment. Then much more softly she said, 'Oh, Roger, if you'd give up Sally – I'd never see him again. I wouldn't even see him tonight.'

CHAPTER FIVE

Around and About the Law

The next day was calmer at No. 1 Temple Court. Mr Grimes was in chambers all day and, except for rushing out for his lunch and rushing back again, his presence in chambers was only noticed by the procession of clients who came for conferences and by the occasional sound of 'Goodbye, my dear fellow, bye, bye, bye' as he saw one or two of the more valued clients to the door. In consequence, Roger was able to ask Henry a number of questions.

'Tomorrow,' said Henry, 'is an important day. I'm in Court. I have to appear before His Honour Judge Boyle at a County Court. P'raps you'd like to come with me. You won't see anything of County Courts with Grimeyboy.'

'D'you think Mr Grimes would mind?' asked Roger.

'Grimes, not Mr Grimes,' said Henry. 'I meant to tell you about that before. Once you're called you call everyone at the Bar by his surname.'

'Even a QC?'

'Everyone. Even an ex-Attorney-General. The newest recruit to the profession will call the most distinguished of all plain Smith or whatever it is. And, while I'm about it, you might as well know how to talk to a judge – out of Court, I mean, or if you write to him. How would you address Mr Justice Blank if you ran into him in the Strand?'

'Well, I'd obviously be wrong. How should I?'

'Judge. "So sorry, Judge," or "do look where you're going, Judge." If he's in the Court of Appeal, call him Lord Justice.'

'And what about an Official Referee?'

'To be quite honest, I've never spoken to one – after his appointment. I suppose you could say "Official Referee," but it's rather a mouthful. "Your Honour" must be wrong. I don't care for "Sir Hugo" or "sir." No, you've got me there. The best advice is not to talk to them. There are only four anyway, so you should be all right. Now, what else can I do for you?'

'Sure you don't mind?'

'My dear boy, I'm only too delighted. Otherwise I'd have to look at these papers. I tell you, I'm bone idle. I'm delighted to have a good excuse for not working.'

'Well, yesterday I heard the clerk talking to someone on the telephone about something called the two-thirds rule. Something to do with fees, I gathered. Can you tell me what it is?'

'Indeed I can. I feel quite strongly on the subject. We had some pronouncements from a Committee on the subject quite recently. Up till a few years before the war if you or I or Grimes or any junior – you know that barristers are either juniors or QCs, and that a QC has to have a junior?'

'That's just about all I do know.'

'Well, as I was saying, up till a few years before the war, if a junior was led by a QC the junior had to receive two-thirds of the fee charged by the QC. So if you were lucky and led by Carson or F E Smith or someone like that, you might get a fee of 666 guineas for doing a case you'd have been perfectly prepared to do for a hundred, or even less. Doesn't sound very logical, you say?'

'I don't say anything,' said Roger. 'I'm listening. I must say, though, I like the sound of 666 guineas. Have you ever had that?'

'I have not, I regret to say. Well, a few years before the war it was agreed that the two-thirds rule should only apply to a fee of 150 guineas or less. Above that it was to be a matter of arrangement.'

'No more 666,' said Roger, sadly.

'Well, some solicitors were prepared to stick to the old rule. Of course some didn't. But there's worse to come. The Committee I mentioned has suggested that the rule should be abolished altogether. The point about the rule is this. By and large, barristers are not overpaid. Indeed much of their work is underpaid. This two-thirds rule is the cream which, when added to the skim milk, makes milk of a reasonable quality. The Committee, while recognizing that barristers are not paid too much, have said something like this: "This two-thirds rule increases the cost of litigation. If it's abolished, barristers will have nothing to make up for the lowness of their other fees, but none the less let's abolish it and good luck to you all." '

'What's going to happen?'

'If you ask me, nothing, but we shall see, my dear fellow, we shall see.'

At that moment Alec came into the room, took away the papers which were in front of Roger and replaced them with a large bundle.

'Mr Grimes thinks you'd better look at these,' he said, and went out again. The brief he left was about six to eight inches thick. Roger looked at it for a moment.

'D'you think I'll ever be able to cope with anything of this kind?' he asked. 'It makes me despair just to look at it.'

'Well,' said Henry, 'it all depends. If you take to the job and are good enough for it, you'll be able to tackle anything in due course. But it'll take time. Let's hope you only get little stuff to begin with. Otherwise you could come a nasty cropper. When I started I made the most awful bloomer with a case. The solicitors took it away from me in the end, but not before I'd done a lot of damage. Think of a medical student being allowed to play at pulling out a patient's appendix and grabbing hold of the wrong thing! I don't even know now whether I was stopped in time. As I said before, it's funny that we're allowed to do it. It's true that the public can't come to us direct as they can to doctors. But there are plenty of Uncle Georges in the world of solicitors – father Georges even – and, of course, brother Georges – their wretched clients don't know that it's your first brief.'

'But,' said Roger, 'one has to start some time. Every professional man has to have his first case, whether it's a doctor, accountant or a barrister.'

'Yes,' said Henry, 'that's true enough, but all professional men, except barristers, have had practical experience first. If a barrister couldn't address the Court until he's had, say, a year as a pupil, that'd be reasonable. Jolly good experience for you yesterday, but what about the poor client?'

'I hope he wasn't there,' said Roger.

'Of course,' said Henry, 'Peter ought to have been doing it, but he wouldn't really have been any better than you. Worse, probably. He'd have talked nonsense; you only said nothing. Neither of you ought to have been allowed to do it, but there you are, my dear fellow, they will do these things, they will do these things.'

'Was I what you call "devilling"?' asked Roger.

'Well,' said Henry, 'if looking unhappy and saying nothing can be called devilling, you were.'

'I suppose,' said Roger, 'that that's what Gilbert was referring to when he said:

"Pocket a fee with a grin on your face
When you haven't been there to attend to the case." '

'Yes,' said Henry, 'but it isn't entirely fair to the Bar to put it just like that. A chap can't be in two places at once and he can't tell when he first accepts a brief in a case that it's going to clash with any other. So there are times when he's got to get help from someone else. All I say is that pupils shouldn't be allowed to give it. Your case is certainly an extreme one and I don't suppose it has happened before or will happen again, but the principle is just the same. No offence to you, but during the whole of your year you won't be capable of handling a defended case in the High Court efficiently, even if you've read it thoroughly.'

'Then why didn't Grimes ask you to help him?' asked Roger.

'Well,' said Henry, 'that could be a long story, but I'll make it a short one. In a nutshell, I've got too big for my boots and I won't devil a brief unless I do the whole thing, or at any rate get half the fee.'

'Look,' said Roger, 'I don't mean to be rude, but you tell me an awful lot. How am I to know you're right?'

'Good for you,' said Henry. 'You can't know. And you're quite right to ask. Go on asking. Don't take anything for granted, not even Grimeyboy. In a month or two you'll think everything he says and does is right.'

'Isn't it?'

'It doesn't matter whether it is or it isn't, you'll think it is. Almost every pupil swears by his master. And it's often quite a long time before he realizes that his written work was bad, that he was only a very moderate lawyer and a poor advocate. I'm not saying any of that about Grimeyboy. It wouldn't in fact be true. But the point is, you must judge for yourself. Ask "why" the whole time. Oh, hullo, Peter. How's the Old Bailey? You know that Thursby had to devil for you yesterday?'

'Thanks very much,' said Peter. 'I'll give you half my fee. Quite a good assault case, as a matter of fact. I'd have been sorry to have missed that. Oh, and there's a good one in the Court of Criminal Appeal tomorrow, I'm told.'

'D'you think I could go?' asked Roger.

'You certainly could,' said Henry, 'and if you want to become like Peter, I should. But if you're wise you'll get on with your work here. Popping off to the Old Bailey or the Court of Criminal Appeal to get a cheap thrill won't teach you anything.'

'I may decide to go to the Criminal Bar,' said Peter.

'If I were you, I should,' said Henry. 'Now I must go and work for once.'

Henry went to his room and Roger started to open a set of papers.

'Don't feel much like work this morning,' said Peter. 'Had a bit of a night last night. What are you reading?'

'I haven't started really,' said Roger. 'This is something called Biggs and Pieman.'

'Oh, that's quite amusing. Pieman's the MP, you know. It'll never come into Court. It's a sort of woman scorned action. Neither side can afford to fight it. Wish they would. It'd be great fun. She's a very attractive woman. I saw her in the clerk's room before she saw Grimeyboy.'

'What's it about?'

'Well – it's a claim for money lent. To judge from the letters, Mrs Biggs and Mr Pieman used to see more of one another than they ought to have done – seeing that there was a Mr Biggs. Well, Pieman apparently needed money to start him on his political career and Mrs B provided it. How much of it was Mr B's I don't know. Later on when the good ship Pieman was firmly launched he broke it off with Mrs B. She was very angry and asked for her money back. He wouldn't pay. So she sued him. He says it's a gift.'

'When is it coming on for trial?'

'I tell you, it isn't. Mr B doesn't know anything about it, but if it came into Court he soon would. There are things in those letters most husbands wouldn't approve of. You read them. They're grand fun. She wanted to know if the action could be heard *in camera*. Of course it couldn't. So it's only a question of who'll give in first. Wouldn't do Pieman any good for his constituency to know that he'd been financed by another man's wife. Wouldn't do her any good for her husband to know she's been so very kind to Mr P. Now, what else is there?'

Peter looked casually at the briefs lying on the table. He picked up one, opened it and read a little, put it back in its red tape and sighed.

'How can anyone be expected to get up any enthusiasm for drawing pins? Consignments of drawing pins. I ask you.'

He picked up another set of papers.

'This isn't much better,' he said. 'It's about wallpaper. I wish he'd have a breach of promise or an enticement action. He hardly ever does a divorce case. Had one the other day, though. Not bad at all. Cruelty case.'

He paused for a moment, trying to recollect some of the more lurid details.

'D'you know, he used to tie her up to a chair and then make faces at her. Now, what would he get out of that?'

'I can't think,' said Roger, but he said it in a tone which caused Peter to say: 'Sorry, old boy. Don't want to interrupt. Think I'll go down to the Old Bailey. Where's Charles?'

'I haven't seen him this morning.'

'Oh, of course. He's got a judgment summons somewhere.'

'What's that?'

'Oh – a summons for debt, you know. I'm not quite sure actually, but you get an Order sending them to prison if they don't pay, or something.'

'I thought that was abolished years ago.'

'So did I, old boy, but it's something like that. You ask Henry. He knows all the answers. Pity he's got no guts. Might have done well. Well, so long, old boy. May not see you again till tomorrow. Depends what they've on at the Old Bailey. I'll take my robes. Might get a docker.'

'A what?'

'Dock brief. You know, surely. I did before I was called. Any prisoner who's got a couple of guineas and the clerk's fee can choose any counsel sitting in Court. So if you just go and sit there you may get a brief. Look hard at the prisoner and hope you hypnotize him into choosing you. Henry's got a good story about dock briefs.'

'What's that?'

'Well, I might as well tell you first. Don't often get in in front of Henry. Well, there was an old lag down at the Bailey. He'd been there dozens of times, knew the ropes. Well, he was up one day for something and decided he'd like to have counsel to defend him. So he brought out his money and they took him up into the dock before the Recorder.

' "Can I have a dock brief, please, my Lord?" he asked, very politely.

48

' "Has he two pounds four shillings and sixpence?" asked the Recorder. The clerk informed the Recorder that the money was there.

' "Very well," said the Recorder. "Choose whom you like," and he pointed to the two rows of counsel sitting in Court. Some were very young, like me, and couldn't have had any experience. Others were very old and moth-eaten. At least one had a hearing aid.

' "What!" said the old lag in horror. "One of those?"

'The Recorder looked at the two rows of counsel and then said rather mournfully: "Yes, I'm afraid so. That's all we have in stock at the moment." '

'Well,' said Roger, 'I wish you luck. But if you did get a brief, would you know what to do with it?'

'As much as anyone else, old boy. Just get up and spout to the jury. Can't come to much harm. They're all guilty. So it doesn't really matter what happens. Feather in your cap if you get them off. Inevitable if they're convicted.'

'I wonder they bother to try them,' said Roger.

'Must go through the motions, old boy,' said Peter. 'And anyway, where would the legal profession be? Justice must not only be done but must appear to be done and, may I add, must be paid for being done. Bye, bye, old boy. Hope you like Mrs Biggs' letters. Some of them are a bit hot. I tried a bit on one of my girlfriends. Went down very well. Breach of copyright, I suppose. But who cares? So long.'

For the next hour Roger was left alone and he devoted himself to the study of *Biggs (married woman) v Pieman*. He found it enthralling – not so much in the way that Peter did, but because he felt so important to be looking into the intimate affairs of other people and, in particular, people of some prominence. Here he was, only just called to the Bar, and he knew things about a Member of Parliament which hardly anyone else knew. And then, supposing by one of those extraordinary coincidences that do take place, he happened to meet Mr Biggs! He might be a member of his uncle's club. And suppose his uncle introduced him and they had dinner together. He'd have to listen while Biggs extolled the virtues of his wife.

'A sweet little woman, though I say it myself who shouldn't,' Mr Biggs might say.

'I don't know whether you should or you shouldn't,' Roger would think to himself. 'Fortunately you didn't say good little woman.' Mr Biggs would go on: 'Pretty as a picture – but I'd trust her with anyone. It's not everyone who can say that, these days.'

'Indeed not,' Roger would think. 'Not with accuracy, anyway.'

At that moment, Mr Grimes came into the pupils' room.

'How are ye, my dear fellow? What are ye looking at? Oh, dear, dear, dear. That kettle of fish. Well, the fellows will be fellows and the girls will be girls. They will do these things, they will do these things.'

'D'you think the action will come into Court?'

'Oh, dear me no, my dear fellow. We can't have that, can we? Dear, dear, dear. Our husband doesn't know of our goings on and we don't want him to. We don't want him to, my dear fellow.'

'Then why did she bring the action?'

'Just a try on, my dear fellow, just a try on. He might have paid up. You can never tell, my dear fellow, you can never tell. There's only one motto I know of that's any good. "Never go to law," my dear fellow, "never go to law". And then where should *we* be, my dear fellow? We shouldn't, should we? So it's just as well they will do these things, isn't it, my dear fellow, just as well.'

Then Alec came in.

'Can you see Mr Wince, sir? He was just passing and wanted to have a word with you about Cooling and Mallet.'

Mr Grimes immediately left the pupils' room. It was not far enough to run but he went as fast as he could. Roger imagined that he would be pretty good at getting to the bathroom first in a boarding house.

'And how's Mr Wince?' Roger heard him say. 'How's Mr Wince today? Come along in, my dear fellow, come along in,' and then Mr Grimes' door closed and Roger heard no more. He wondered what Mr Wince wanted. What was Cooling and Mallet about? He looked on his table. What a piece of luck. There it was. He quickly tied up the bundle he had been reading and opened Cooling and Mallet. At that moment Alec came in.

'Mr Grimes wants these, I'm afraid, sir,' he said and took them away.

Roger went back to the sins of Mr Pieman and Mrs Biggs. Even at his age he found it a little sad to see how the attitude between men and women can change. The letters, which in the early correspondence started and ended so very, very affectionately, full of all the foolish-looking but (to them) sweet sounding endearments of lovers, gradually cooled off. 'My dearest, sweetest turnip, how I adore you' became 'Dear Mr Pieman, if I do not receive a cheque by return I shall place the matter in other hands.' Is it really possible that I could ever hate the sight of Joy or Sally as undoubtedly Mr Pieman now hates the sight of Mrs Biggs? Perhaps it only happens, he thought, when the relationship has been that of husband and wife, or worse. At twenty-one these things are a little difficult to understand.

Roger had an hour more with Mr Pieman and Mrs Biggs when Charles returned. The Court he had attended was some way away, but he was still hot and flushed.

'Hullo,' said Roger. 'How did you get on? I hear you've been doing a judgment something or other. I wish you'd tell me about it.'

'I wish you'd asked me that yesterday. Then I might have had to look it up. As it is, I have lost my one and only client.'

'I'm so sorry. What happened?' asked Roger sympathetically.

'I'd learned the ruddy thing by heart. There wasn't a thing I didn't know.' He broke off. 'It really is too bad.'

'Do tell me, unless you'd rather not.'

'I think I'd like to get it off my chest. I was doing a js – a judgment summons. That's an application to send to prison a person who hasn't paid a judgment debt, but you can only succeed if you can prove he has had the means to pay the debt or at any rate, part of it since the judgment. The debtor has to attend and my job was to cross-examine him for all I was worth to show that he could have paid. I went to the Court with my client and I told him the sort of questions I was going to ask and he seemed very impressed. "That'll shake him," he said several times. I was really feeling confident. And what d'you think happened? The case was called on and the chap didn't turn up. Well, that was bad enough, but it was after that that the trouble really began. After all, I can't know everything, can I, and I *had* read that brief. If the chap had been there I'd have knocked him to bits. But he wasn't. "Well," said the judge, "what do you want me to do?" Well, I ought to have looked it up, I suppose, but I hadn't. I'd no idea what I wanted him to do. Fortunately my client knew more than

I did. "Have him fined," he whispered. "Would Your Honour fine him?" I said.

' "Your client wants his money, I suppose," said the judge. "What good will fining him do?"

'I had no idea. Again my client prompted me. "If he doesn't pay, he goes to prison."

'I repeated this to the judge.

' "But surely that isn't right," said the judge. "You've got to prove means before he goes to prison."

' "Not in the case of a fine," whispered my client.

' "Not in the case of a fine, Your Honour," I repeated, like the good parrot I had become.

'I was already beginning to feel extremely small, particularly after the exhibition I'd given to my client in the train as to what I was going to do with this judgment debtor. Here I was, just repeating what he was feeding me with. But even that wouldn't have been so bad if it had been right.

' "Nonsense," said the judge. "You can't commit a man for non-payment of a fine unless you can prove he has the means to pay. Do you know what is meant by an argument in a circle?"

' "I think so, Your Honour," I said.

' "A good example," said the judge, "is the law relating to judgment summonses. If a judgment debt isn't paid, the debtor can only be sent to prison if you can prove he has had the means to pay. Usually you can't do that unless he's present to be cross-examined about his means. If he doesn't obey the summons to appear, he can be fined, but you can't do anything about the fine unless you can prove he has the means to pay it. But he doesn't come. So you can't ask him questions or prove anything. So you're back where you started. Of course, if he's got any goods on which distress can be levied, it's different, but then you'd have tried execution and wouldn't have bothered about a judgment summons in that case."

'Meantime I'm standing there, getting red in the face.

' "Well, Mr Hepplewhite, what would you like me to do?"

'Someone in the row – a barrister or solicitor – whispered to me. "Ask for a 271."

'Again I did as suggested.

' "What on earth's that?" asked the judge.

'Well, what could I say? The chap next to me might have been pulling my leg. I didn't know. I didn't know anything. So I said so. You can hardly blame the judge.

' "Really," he said. "This is too bad. Summons dismissed."

'My client said something to me about looking up the rules another time and added that he wouldn't be coming back my way. On the way home I started looking it up – and, blow me, if there isn't a thing called a 271. The chap was quite right. It was the only thing to do. Even the judge didn't know it. It's certainly a lesson to look up the rules another time. But it takes it out of you, a thing like that.'

'It must have been awful,' said Roger. 'But you can't look up everything before you go into Court,' he went on. 'How d'you know what to look up?'

'Well, I suppose,' said Charles, 'if you have a judgment summons, you ought to look up the rules which govern them. And I suppose, too, one ought to visualize the possibility of a man not turning up and find out what you can do then. I shan't forget 271 in a hurry. I feel like writing to the judge about it. After all, he ought to have known it.'

'What is a 271?' asked Roger.

'It's an authority to arrest the debtor and bring him before the Court if he doesn't pay a fine within the time he's been given to pay it. So it isn't an argument in a circle. You can get the debtor there. Funny the judge didn't know.'

'I suppose there are things judges don't know,' said Roger, 'Henry's got a case in a County Court tomorrow. D'you think it would be a good thing if I went with him? He said I could.'

'I should. You'll learn a lot from Henry. And, apart from that, he'll tell you stories on the way. He's got an unending fund of them. And they'll all be new to *you*. I expect that's one of the reasons he asked you to come.'

Roger spent the rest of the day reading the papers in *Biggs v Pieman* and the case about drawing pins. The evening he spent with Sally.

'It's amazing to think what's going on and no one knows it. I saw a case today about a Member of Parliament.'

'Who?'

'Oh, I couldn't tell you that. One of the first things Grimes told me was that anything I learn I must treat with confidence.'

'Then why did you tell me about the case at all?'

'You couldn't possibly identify the parties.'

'What's it about then?'

'Well, I suppose there can't be any harm in that. There are over six hundred MPs and an infinite variety of married women.'

So Roger told her the facts as well as he remembered them.

'Humph!' said Sally. 'It *is* quite interesting. Sounds like old Pieman. I wouldn't put it past him.'

'What did you say?' said Roger, so horrified that he was unable to stop himself from asking the question, or from showing in his voice the surprise he felt.

'Roger – it is – it's old Pieman. Mother will be thrilled.'

'Sally, you're not to.'

'Then it is. How extraordinary.'

'The other thing I was looking at,' said Roger, lamely, 'was about drawing pins.'

'It's much too late now, Roger. I know all about it.'

'Sally, you mustn't tell anyone. Promise you won't.'

'You didn't tell me in confidence, Roger.'

'But I learned it in confidence.'

'Then you shouldn't have told me in the first instance. Now, let's think who I've seen about with old Pieman.'

'Sally, you mustn't. How was I to know you knew him?'

'How were you to know I didn't.'

'I never thought for a moment – oh, Sally, please promise you won't tell anyone. I've done the most terrible thing.'

'I know who it is,' said Sally. 'A very smart woman – now what's her name? Let me think.'

'Please, Sally, please. I'm sure it isn't, anyway.'

'How can you possibly tell? I know, Anstruther, that's the name, Mollie Anstruther.'

'No,' said Roger.

'Roger,' said Sally, 'I'm sorry to have to tell you this – I do it more in sorrow than in anger and all for your own good – but it'll hurt you more than it hurts me all the same – you're an ass – an unmitigated ass. Why on earth did you say "no" when I mentioned Mollie Anstruther? That eliminates one possibility. Now I can try to think of someone else. I thought that was the sort of trick barristers played on other people.'

'Well, I didn't think it would be fair on the woman to let you think it was her.'

'Then it must be Dorothy Biggs. I've often seen them about together.'

Roger said nothing for a moment. Then: 'How on earth could I tell you'd guess?' he said miserably.

'What'll you do if I promise not to tell anyone?'

'I'll be more careful in future.'

'Is that all? You'll do that anyway, I hope.'

'There won't be any necessity. If you go telling people about it, it'll quite likely become known that it came out through me and then I shall be disbarred. After three days, too. I'm in your hands, Sally.'

'Don't be silly,' said Sally. 'Of course I shan't tell anyone.'

'You're a darling. I don't know what I should do without you.'

'Well, you'd have told someone else, I suppose.'

'Yes, I suppose I should. I am an ass. You're quite right, Sally. How lucky it was you.'

'Well,' said Sally thoughtfully, 'Joy might not have known the parties – but if she had – I'm sure she'd have done just what I did. Wouldn't she, Roger?'

'Yes,' said Roger, uncomfortably, 'I'm sure she would.'

'Well, that's settled,' said Sally brightly. 'Now you're going to tell me about the drawing pins.'

'They were in confidence, Sally. You might have sat on one of them.'

'Too true,' said Sally. 'And does this mean that you're never going to tell me anything?'

'Of course not. I can tell you anything that happens in Court. And I can tell you about the people in chambers. Old Grimes is an extraordinary person. But he's got the most tremendous practice. And I gather his clients swear by him.'

'From what you told me yesterday on the phone, I thought you did most of his work for him.'

'I didn't put it as high as that. Oh, by the way, tomorrow I'm going to a County Court with an awfully nice chap called Henry Blagrove. He's quite brilliant, I think, but I haven't heard him in Court yet.'

'What's a County Court? Where they fine you for not having dog licences?'

'Oh, no. It's a Court for trying small civil cases – breaches of contracts, debts, accident cases and so on. And they have things called judgment summonses there. D'you know, they still send people to prison for not paying debts. I must say I thought that had been abolished after *Pickwick Papers.*'

'Are there debtors' prisons still then?'

'I don't think so. They go to ordinary prisons, I think. As a matter of fact, I don't believe many people actually go to prison. About a thousand a year, I was told.'

'I must ask mother,' said Sally. 'She sings at prisons sometimes.'

'That is good of her,' said Roger. 'She must go down awfully well. They like almost anything there – I mean, I mean – '

'Explain it to mother,' said Sally, 'here she is.'

Mrs Mannering came into the room a moment later.

'How are you, Roger? How nice of you to take tickets for Friday. I'm sure you can't afford it, as a poor struggling barrister.'

'I've been looking forward to hearing you,' said Roger. 'I was only saying so to Sally a moment ago.'

'How sweet of you. Walter Burr's going to accompany me. I've made him promise not to say a word. He's a brilliant accompanist but he's suddenly got the idea that he's a comedian too. And he always tries to introduce the songs and do a comic turn at the same time. Seems catching in the musical profession at the moment. Oh, who do you think gave me a lift home, wasn't it kind? Walter Pieman – the MP, you know. I met him at Hilda's.'

Roger and Sally said nothing for a moment. Then Sally said, 'It only goes to show, doesn't it?'

'Goes to show what?' said her mother.

'That MPs have their uses.'

The next day Roger met Henry at a tube station on the way to the County Court.

'I see you've a red bag,' said Roger. 'Have you had it long?'

'I was lucky,' said Henry. 'I got a brief with a leader in my second year and somehow or other it produced this. Lucky. It's much lighter than carrying a suitcase, particularly if you've got a lot of books to take.'

'But why a suitcase?'

'Well – after a few years some people don't like to be seen with a blue bag. So they use a suitcase instead.'

'Who gave you yours?'

'Mostyn, as a matter of fact.'

'I say, that's awfully good, isn't it? He's one of the biggest leaders now, isn't he?'

'Well, he's made a lot of headway in the last year or two. Yes, I was lucky. Curiously enough, I actually earned it. I worked like hell.'

'Don't people always earn them?'

'As often as not it's done between the clerks. George meets Ernest in the "Cock." "D'you think you could get young Bolster a red bag, Ernie?" he says over the third pint. "I'll try, old boy," says Ernest. And if Ernest tries the answer is probably "yes." It's a funny custom. The only people who make anything out of it really are the people who make the bags. But it's a sort of milestone in a chap's career. The day he gets his red bag. You certainly won't find your way to the Woolsack without one.'

They discussed the other milestones in a career at the Bar; then they talked about County Courts.

'What's this judge like?' asked Roger.

'Well, fortunately,' said Henry, 'there aren't any others like him today. I don't mean by that that he's a bad judge. He isn't. But he's very inconsiderate. Furthermore, he's peppery, pompous and conceited, but he's quite a good judge for all that, though not as good as he thinks he is. Incidentally, one of the funniest things I ever heard happened in front of him. Like to hear?'

'That's one of the reasons I've come,' said Roger.

'Charles told you that, I suppose,' said Henry, and they both laughed.

There were three main characters in the story which Henry told Roger. The first was a barrister called Galloway, a well-intentioned, very serious and literally-minded man. The second was a former County Court judge called Musgrave.

'He's dead now,' said Henry. 'He was a nice old boy and quite a good judge when he tried a case, but he was a wicked old man and wouldn't sit after lunch. There aren't any others like him today, either.'

'What d'you mean?' asked Roger.

'What I say. He wouldn't sit after lunch. He spent part of the morning either making people settle cases or adjourning them for one reason or another and finally he tried what was left and rose at lunchtime. Very rarely he came back after lunch, but, usually he made some excuse for postponing any case which hadn't finished by lunchtime until another day. I liked him, but he certainly was naughty. Well, one day Galloway had a case in front of Musgrave. It was an accident case which would have been likely to occupy a considerable part of the day. The judge had a medical referee sitting beside him to advise. When I say sitting, well, it was arranged that he should sit. The only question in the case was whether a man's illness had been caused by the accident, but a good deal of evidence would have had to be given about it. Before the judge sat he sent for the doctors who were being called on each side and told them to have a word with the medical referee. After they'd had a chat for ten minutes or so, the judge went in to see them himself. Five minutes later he came into Court, sat down and announced that there would be judgment in the case for the defendants with costs.

' "But – " said the unfortunate Galloway, who was appearing for the plaintiff.

' "But what?" said the judge, quite severely.

' "But – " repeated Galloway.

' "If that's all you have to say, Mr Galloway, I'll have the next case called," and this was duly done.

'Well, of course, the plaintiff wasn't going to take that lying down. His case had never been tried. The judge had no doubt acted upon what the doctors had told him behind closed doors. It was a complete denial of justice. So the plaintiff appealed to the Court of Appeal and Galloway started to tell their Lordships all about it. He hadn't gone very far with the story before the president of the Court, Lord Justice Brand, said: "It's very difficult to believe that this really happened. Naturally, I'm not doubting your word, Mr Galloway, but how can it have happened as you say without your saying something to the judge?"

' "I did say something, my Lord."

' "Oh – what was that?"

' " 'But,' my Lord."

' "Yes, Mr Galloway?"

' " 'But,' my Lord."

' "But what, Mr Galloway?"

' "Just 'but,' my Lord."

' "I'm afraid I'm out of my depth," said another Lord Justice. "Are you still addressing us, Mr Galloway?"

' "Yes, my Lord."

' "Then what did you mean when you said 'but' to my brother?"

' "That was what I said, my Lord."

' "I know you did, twice. But why?"

' "I couldn't think of anything else to say, my Lord."

' "Now, look," said Lord Justice Brand. "Let us get this straight. You didn't say 'but' to us – ?"

' "Oh, yes, he did," said Lord Justice Rowe.

' "I know, I know," said Lord Justice Brand. "Please let me finish. The 'but' you said to us was the 'but' you said to the learned County Court judge, or to put it more accurately, it was another 'but' but the same word. 'But' is what you said to the County Court judge."

' "Yes, my Lord," said Galloway.

'Lord Justice Brand sat back in his chair triumphantly.

' "But," said Lord Justice Rowe, "if I may be forgiven the use of the word, but is that all you said to the learned judge?"

' "Yes, my Lord, just 'but.' "

' "But it doesn't mean anything."

' "I didn't get a chance to say anything more, my Lord, and I was too flabbergasted."

' "Really, Mr Galloway," said Lord Justice Brand. "When I was at the Bar, I considered it to be my duty in the interests of my client to stand up to the judge and, if necessary, to be rude to him, yes, to be rude to him. I cannot believe that counsel of your experience would allow a thing like that to happen unchallenged."

'In the end, of course, they allowed the appeal and sent the case back to the County Court to be properly heard before another judge, but not before poor Galloway's mildness had been further criticized.

'A week later he had an accident case before Boyle – the judge you're going to meet. Galloway was appearing for the plaintiff. He got up and started to open the case to the jury, explaining to them where the accident happened and so on. He was just saying: "Now, members of the jury, at that juncture the defendant's car without any warning of any kind whatsoever – " when the judge interrupted: "Mr Galloway, might I have a plan, please?"

' "Be quiet," said Galloway and continued to address the jury. "And without any warning of any kind whatsoever – "

'Just as the Court of Appeal could not believe what was said to have happened in Musgrave's Court, Boyle couldn't believe he'd heard Galloway aright. Galloway was a polite man and his behaviour was normally impeccable.

' "I really can't follow this without a plan," said Boyle.

' "Will you be quiet," said Galloway and started to go on addressing the jury. But not for long. This time the judge had no doubt what had been said.

' "Have you taken leave of your senses, Mr Galloway?" he said angrily. "How dare you speak to me like that!"

' "Well, your Honour," said Galloway. "I was told last week by the Court of Appeal that it was my duty to be rude to the judge." '

CHAPTER SIX

His Honour Judge Boyle

They arrived at the Court in plenty of time and went straight to the robing-room. It was crowded with solicitors and counsel.

'Hullo, Henry, are we against one another?' said a middle-aged barrister.

'I don't know. I'm in – now what's the name of it? Wait a minute, I can never remember.'

He opened his bag and got out the brief. 'Oh, yes, of course, Swift and Edgerley.'

'Yes, that's me,' said the other. 'We've got a hope. We're about last. He's got some judgment summonses, half a dozen possession cases and three other actions before ours. Any use asking him to let us go?'

'Not a chance,' said Henry. 'But all the same I should think we'd better try. The old so-and-so will never let anyone get away before lunch. I think he likes an audience really, to hear his wise remarks and his quotations from Birkenhead's famous judgment. Is anyone else going to have a crack at it? Let's get in before he sits and see what the form is.'

Counsel's and solicitors' row made an impressive sight for His Honour Judge Boyle as he walked on to the Bench. Henry was right in thinking that he liked an audience. The judge moved in and sat down slowly. He was a heavy man and not young. The first thing he did was to look at the pencils. He obviously did not approve of them. He tapped on his desk for the clerk to speak to him.

'Take these beastly things away,' he said, 'and get me some decent ones. I can't use those. How many more times have I got to say so?'

'I'm sorry, your Honour,' said the clerk.

'It's not your fault,' grunted the judge. 'It's what they send us. I've complained about it dozens of times. They'll expect me to write with my thumbnail next.'

The clerk sent out for some more pencils.

A solicitor got up: 'Might I mention to your Honour,' he began.

'No, not yet,' said the judge irritably. The solicitor sat down with a sigh.

'Cheerful mood today,' whispered one member of the Bar to another.

'The old idiot. I'd like to chuck the lot at him.'

'If people want to talk they must go outside,' said the judge.

'Charming,' said Henry, but quietly enough.

The new pencils were brought. The judge tried them. 'I suppose they'll have to do,' he said eventually. 'They're better than the last. Thank you, Mr Jones.'

'Shall I call the first application, your Honour?'

'Yes, please.'

'Mrs Turner,' called the clerk, and a small woman went into the witness box. She was making an application for some money to be paid out to her from a fund in Court. She was a widow whose husband had been killed some years before in an accident and the Court controlled her use of the damages she had been awarded.

'Well,' said the judge, after glancing at the papers in front of him, 'what do you want £10 for?'

He asked her as though she were a beggar at the back door when she was, in fact, the owner of the fund in Court. It was her money, but the Court had the paternal duty of seeing that she did not expend it too foolishly. The judge's manner was not in the least paternal.

'Please, your Worship,' the woman began –

'She's had it,' whispered a solicitor, 'calling him your worship.'

'It's a first payment for a television set.'

The judge's eyes gleamed. His remarks about television and other abominations of the modern age had frequently been reported in the Press.

'A television set,' he growled. 'What on earth d'you want with one of those things? Read a good book and get it from the library. Cost you nothing.'

'Please, your Worship, I can't read, not really.'

'What on earth have we been paying taxes for all these years? It's disgraceful.'

'Please, your Worship, I'm nearly blind.'

'Oh, I'm sorry,' said the judge. He thought for a moment and then added in a more kindly tone: 'But is a television set much use to you then? Why not have a wireless instead?'

'Oh, I have a wireless, your Worship.'

'I see.'

The judge hesitated.

'You think you'll get some pleasure out of a television set, do you?'

'Oh, yes, your Worship. Mrs Crane across the road has one and she can't see a thing.'

'Perhaps it's an advantage then,' said the judge. 'Yes, very well, Mrs Turner. You shall have your television set. Ten pounds I think you want. Very well. Can you pay the instalments all right? Good. They'll give you your money in the office. I hope your sight improves.'

'Might I now mention to your Honour,' began the solicitor who had tried before, hoping that the shock which the judge had just received might have put him in a more receptive mood.

'Certainly not,' said the judge just as fiercely as before, but not quite for the same reason. He was visualizing Mrs Turner's life without her husband and without much sight. 'And probably she hasn't much to think with either,' he was pondering, 'though p'raps it's as well,' when the solicitor had interrupted.

'Mr Copplestone,' called the clerk, and a young man went into the witness box. The judge glared at him. He had already glanced at his application.

'A motor bicycle,' he said. 'One of those horrible things. Why don't you use a pedal cycle or walk? Much better for you and safer. You'll go and kill yourself.'

'I'm getting married,' ventured the young man.

'You'll kill your wife too,' said the judge.

'I'm twenty-one next month,' said the young man, 'and we wanted the bike for our honeymoon.'

This was a young man who had been awarded damages when he was a small boy. At the age of twenty-one he would be entitled to all of it, but until then the Court had control.

'Why can't you wait?' asked the judge. He knew he couldn't keep the young man away from a motor bicycle for long, but he did not want to be a party to the transaction.

'We don't want to, your Honour.'

'I dare say you don't. Have you your parents' permission?'

'To have the bike, your Honour?'

67

'No, of course not. No one asks parents' permission for anything these days. You just go and do it. No – to marry, I mean. Still need it for that.'

'Can I speak?' said a man from the back of the Court.

'Silence,' called the usher.

'But it's all wrong,' shouted the man.

'Silence,' called the usher even louder.

'Let that man be brought forward,' commanded the judge. He required no bringing forward and came hastily to the witness box.

'Who are you?' asked the judge.

'I'm his father,' said the man. 'And I think it's a shame.'

'You've already interrupted the proceedings twice and if you speak like that I shall deal with you for contempt of Court. You'll either speak properly or not at all. Now, what is it you want to say?'

'I say, give the boy his bike. Why spoil the young people's pleasure? You only get married once.'

'Unfortunately,' said the judge, unable to resist the temptation, 'that today is not always the case, though I hope it will be in this instance. But if I let him have this horrible machine one of them at least will probably be killed.'

'They can't afford a car,' said the man. 'And they don't want to go for a honeymoon by bus or train. They want to be with each other. And I say they ought to be. My old woman and I went walking, but then we didn't have the luck to have had an accident and get the damages. Though it doesn't look as though that's going to be much good to him.'

'Will you be quiet,' said the judge.

'Why doesn't the Registrar do these?' whispered Henry to his opponent.

68

'Because the old fool likes doing them. He ought to do them in chambers, anyway. Pompous old idiot. Doesn't care two hoots how much time he takes up or how much he inconveniences everyone.'

The judge finished his applications, having very grudgingly given the young man his money. He realized that it would not be fair in this instance to refuse it.

'Now, does anyone want to mention any of the cases?'

The solicitor had a third attempt.

'Any member of the Bar,' asked the judge, ignoring the solicitor.

Henry's opponent got up.

'Your Honour is always so exceedingly considerate that I'm prompted to ask leave to mention the last case in your Honour's list,' he said.

'Let me see,' said the judge, 'Swift and Edgerley, is that it?'

'Yes, your Honour. My learned friend, Mr Blagrove, and I were wondering whether your Honour would give any indication of whether that case is likely to be heard today. I would not have mentioned the matter but your Honour is always so exceedingly helpful in these matters and as there are seven cases in front of us – ' he paused and waited to see what effect his piece of hypocrisy had had.

'One does one's best, Mr Tate,' said the judge, 'but, as you know, it's very difficult with such heavy lists. Would it be a convenience to you if I said that I would not hear your case before the luncheon adjournment?'

'No bloody use at all,' said Tate in an undertone to Henry. 'Thank you very much, your Honour,' he went on. 'That is most kind of your Honour. Perhaps we might have leave to mention the matter again after the adjournment.'

'Certainly, Mr Tate.'

'If your Honour pleases,' beamed Mr Tate. 'The old so-and-so,' he added to Henry, 'he knows bloody well we can't get back to the Temple from here.'

'Any other applications from the Bar?' asked the judge. There was no response.

'Now, Mr Bloat, what is your application?'

'Would your Honour release my case too until after lunch?'

'If I release every case I shall have nothing to do. Are there any other applications?'

'But, your Honour – ' began Mr Bloat.

'What is it, Mr Bloat?' said the judge angrily. 'It's quite impossible for me to help the parties in these matters if they don't accept my decision when I've given it. I do the best I can.'

'I think you're brilliant,' said Henry to Tate when they were in the robing-room again. 'It would stick in my gullet to talk to the old boy like that.'

'When you're my age,' said Tate, 'you'll never mind saying "please" to anyone if it'll get you anywhere or anything – even if you think you oughtn't to have had to ask for it – indeed, even if it's your own. It costs nothing and sometimes it gets something. At any rate we can have a smoke and plenty of time for lunch. He only rises for half an hour.'

'But you perjured your immortal soul in the process.'

'If you feel so strongly on the subject, my boy,' said Tate, 'you should have got up and disagreed when I said the old fool was so exceedingly helpful. See how far that would have got us! Anyway by keeping silent you adopted my lie and cannot now be heard to complain of it. Estopped, my boy, that's what you are. And when you get before St Peter, he'll have you for that. "You told a lie to His Honour Judge Boyle," he'll say. You'll start to deny it. "We can't have

70

that," he'll say. "You told a lie to Judge Boyle all right. Good for you. Come inside." '

Eventually Henry's case was heard and he and Roger left the Court together.

'What sort of a clerk is Alec?' Roger asked him.

'Alec has, in my view,' said Henry, 'only one fault. This,' and Henry imitated Alec sucking his teeth so successfully that Roger winced. 'Cheer up – you'll have to get used to that,' said Henry, and did it again. 'Some people,' he went on, 'would say that he had two other faults. He doesn't drink or smoke. But that's a matter of opinion.'

'Clerks seem to be most frightfully important,' said Roger.

'Well, you've noticed something. They are. A top-class man will always get on, but a second-rater could be made or marred by his clerk.'

'How does a clerk begin?'

'Usually as a boy in the Temple, at a very small wage. Then, if he's no good, he goes to something else. If he does take to it, he becomes a junior and then, if he's lucky, a senior clerk. D'you know, Alec was making a thousand a year when he was not much older than you are, and a thousand was a thousand in those days.'

'It's extraordinary. Of course, the method of paying them beats me. I must say I like the idea of having my clerk paid by the clients. Is there any other profession in the world where it happens?'

'I don't know of one – except, of course, that they're really paid by commission and there are plenty of commission jobs. But they are rather different, I suppose. Yes, it is a curious arrangement that every time I have a conference my clerk gets five bob and the client pays him. But, of course, until you've got a practice you'll have to pay him a salary. And they're inclined to take the shillings in the guineas now as well from everyone.'

71

'What do they make these days?'

'Depends entirely on the chambers. But a clerk in a really good set of chambers might make two or three thousand a year, I suppose. And he's never read a law-book in his life, though he's carried a good few. All the same, the work he does is jolly important and the wheels wouldn't go round without him. Getting briefs, fixing up the fees and arranging it so that you're not in too many places at the same time. It takes a bit of doing. An intelligent and experienced clerk earns his keep all right.'

'What I like,' said Roger, 'is the sort of relationship which seems to exist between them and us.'

'Quite right!' said Henry. 'It's quite different from any other. There's an intimacy and understanding between a barrister and his clerk which, as far as I know, doesn't exist in any other job. And neither side ever takes advantage of it. But Heaven preserve me from a bad clerk. Alec does me proud – indeed, he'd do me much better if I'd let him, and I don't mind his little habit as much as you seem to.' And Henry repeated it several times until he saw that it really upset Roger. 'Sorry, old boy,' he said. 'I didn't know you took it to heart so. I'll try to remember,' and he just checked himself from repeating the process.

Shortly afterwards they parted. Henry went home and Roger went back to chambers. When he arrived there, he was greeted by Alec.

'There's a brief been sent down to you, sir, for next Friday.'

'For me?'

'Yes, sir. I thought you might know about it. The solicitors are something Merivale. Someone you know, I expect?'

'Gosh,' said Roger. 'Joy's uncle already.'

CHAPTER SEVEN

First Brief

It was a divorce case. Roger picked it up lovingly. It looked so beautiful in its fresh pink tape with 'Mr Roger Thursby' typed neatly on it and almost as important, the fee – the fee that someone was going to pay him for his services. Seven whole guineas. He had never earned as much before in his life, though he had once earned a few guineas by tutoring a boy advertised as 'Backward (nothing mental).' He was a nice boy with a fiercely obstinate disposition and determined to learn nothing that his parents wanted him taught. He could recognize almost any bird or flower and many tunes from classical music. His parents were not musical, so he used to turn on the Third Programme. Funny, thought Roger, how one train of thought leads to another. Why should I be thinking of Christopher because someone's sent me a brief? A brief. His very own. Mr Roger Thursby. Five and two, total seven. And at the bottom 'Thornton, Merivale & Co, 7 Butts Buildings, EC4. Solicitors for the Petitioner.' The Petitioner. The life and happiness of one man or one woman had been entrusted to him. Man or woman, which was it? The outside of the brief, which was entitled 'In the High Court of Justice. Probate, Divorce and Admiralty Division (Divorce). Newent E v Newent K R,' did not disclose whether the petitioner was to be a beautiful blonde. Perhaps it was an actress – Sally's mother might know her – no, that wouldn't do – it was Joy's uncle who'd sent the brief. What a pity it wasn't Sally's. He'd no business to think that. It was most ungrateful. How kind it was of Joy and she was really very pretty. Or was it a man, an admiral, perhaps, or a general or even a Member of Parliament? Well, he could soon find out. He opened the brief. E stood for Ethel. His first petitioner was a woman. Poor thing! What a brute of a husband! Now she had Roger to protect her. It was Roger Galahad Thursby who looked eagerly at the rest of the papers. At the age of twenty-one Roger found that rescuing ladies (in the imagination) occupied quite a portion of his idle moments. At that age the pictures of such events rather embarrassed him. He preferred her to be fully clothed. Roger started to read the brief and was a little disappointed to find that all that Mr Newent had done was to leave his wife – and, as far as could be ascertained, not even for another woman. Roger made the best of it, however, and soon imagined himself giving his client words of encouragement and consolation which would stem the poor girl's grief. Even this idea was slightly shaken when he found that the poor girl was forty-five and that she was what is called 'asking for the discretion of the Court.' But Roger steeled himself to the task. He was broadminded. He did not in fact approve of infidelity. He had attended several weddings and had always been impressed by the words of the marriage service. He had difficulty in reconciling them with the number of divorces which now take place. But now he was face to face with an unfaithful wife – on paper anyway, and he would soon see her. He could not help feeling a thrill at the prospect. He had never to his knowledge met an – an adulteress before. It was rather a terrible word. The newspapers often covered it up. They talked of misconduct and infidelity. Adulteress sounded much worse. And then he remembered the great words on the subject. 'He that is without sin among you – ' Yes, Roger would speak to this poor, fallen woman in a kindly, understanding way. She would never realize he was only twenty-one. He would speak with such an air of knowledge, such a wealth of understanding, that she would probably cry. And he would say: 'Madam, you and I have only just met – but I think I know what you have been through.' He paused in his thoughts. What next? Ah, yes, more sinned against than sinning. The lonely, slighted wife, devoted to a husband who neglected her for his business and his billiards. There she was alone at home, waiting, waiting – an easy prey for the handsome seducer. Yes, more sinned against than sinning, that was it. He read through the whole brief, the correspondence, the petition and the discretion statement. This last document was the one in which Mrs Newent disclosed how she came to sin and humbly asked the Court – not to forgive her – but to grant a decree of divorce just the same. Mr Newent apparently was quite willing to be divorced and had not even entered an appearance to the petition. This was a pity, thought Roger. It was difficult to make an impassioned speech against someone who wouldn't fight. And it was very clear that Mr Newent wasn't going to fight. His last letter to Ethel went as follows:

Dear Ethel
It is no good asking me to return. I told you when I left that this is final and it is. I had one year of happiness with you and five years of the other thing. You cared much more for your beastly boarding house and some of the boarders than you did for me,

though I shall be surprised if you make more of a success of that business than you did of our marriage. 'Service with a smile' you used to put in your advertisements. Having regard to the charges you made and the little value you gave for them, I should have expected service to be with a smile, not to say a broad grin. If you don't treat your guests better than you treated me you'll lose them too. Most of them, that is. But then some people never learn. I have. And I'm not coming back to 'Sans Repos' – which is what it ought to be called. But you wouldn't understand. You can understand this, though, that I'm not coming back – no never – whether you divorce me or whether you don't. I hope you will because I'd like to be free. Not that I've met anyone else. I'll be darn careful about the next one, believe me. But if I can't be free, at any rate I'll be happy. I don't wish you any harm, Ethel. Maybe there is some man who'd be happy with you, but it's not

Yours

Kenneth

This letter had been written in reply to a very short one by Ethel which had simply said:

I'm writing for the last time to know whether you propose to return to me. If you do not I shall take such action as I may be advised.

The material parts of the discretion statement were as follows:

After I had been married to my husband for some years he ceased to take any interest in my business of

76

a boarding house proprietress, although he knew when we married that I was very keen on my business and wanted to continue with it after marriage. He had agreed to this, but nevertheless he was always asking me to give it up and make a home for him. At last he refused even to look after the accounts, and one of the boarders, who had been with us for some years and who did a little accounting in his spare time, very kindly started to do them for me. As a result of this I got to know this gentleman, a Mr Storrington, rather well. One night he asked me to go to a dance with him, and, as at the time my husband was staying with his parents (one of whom was ill), I did not think there would be any harm in it. We went to a dance and unfortunately I had rather too much to drink. I am not a teetotaller, but very rarely drink intoxicating liquor. During the evening I had several drinks and though I felt all right during the dance, when we left I felt dizzy and faint. Mr Storrington very kindly offered to help me to my bedroom and somehow or other he came in and adultery took place. I felt very ashamed the next morning and told Mr Storrington that it must never happen again or he would have to leave. Mr Storrington promised that it would not occur again. Since my husband left me I have seen more and more of Mr Storrington and an affection has developed between us and, if this Court sees fit to grant me a decree of divorce, I wish to marry Mr Storrington and he is willing to marry me. Although Mr Storrington and I are living in the same house on affectionate terms adultery has not occurred between us except as aforesaid, nor have I committed any act of adultery with any other person. To the best of my

knowledge and belief my husband was and is wholly
unaware of my adultery.

It was a pity in some ways, thought Roger at first, that Mr
Storrington was still about the place. For it meant that the
petitioner already had a companion and friend. But Roger
soon adjusted himself to the new situation, and decided
that the poor little woman who had never known
happiness with her husband should be given a new and
happy life with her new husband, and it would be Roger
who would be responsible for giving it her. After he had
been through the papers several times Roger asked if he
could see Mr Grimes, and eventually Alec managed to
sandwich him in between two conferences.

'Well, my dear fellow, what can I do for ye?'

Roger mentioned that he'd had a brief for the petitioner
in an undefended divorce. Might he ask a few questions
about it?

'Of course, my dear fellow, of course. But ye won't have
any trouble, my dear fellow. Not like it was in the old days.
That was a very different cup of tea, a very different cup of
tea, my dear fellow. Nowadays it's like shelling peas, my
dear chap. In one door and out the other before you can
say "knife." '

'This is what they call a discretion case. Does that make
any difference?'

'Oh, that's all right, my dear fellow, just tell the judge
the tale, tell the judge the tale.'

'As a matter of fact my client committed adultery before
her husband left her. Does that make any difference?'

'Did he know of it, my dear fellow?'

'Oh – no.'

'Then that's all right then, my dear fellow. What the eye
sees not, the heart grieves not.'

'I just wondered if it was desertion for a man to leave his wife if she'd committed adultery.'

'Oh, yes, my dear fellow, so long as he doesn't know, that's desertion all right. You look up *Herod and Herod*. That'll tell you all about it. And there are some later cases in the Court of Appeal. Now is there anything else I can do for you, my dear fellow?'

'No, thank you very much. It's most kind of you.'

'Not at all, my dear fellow. Very glad you've had your first brief. Had to wait much longer in my day. But everything's faster these days. I don't know what we're coming to. Judges on the Bench that haven't been called twenty years. I don't know, my dear fellow, I don't know. But there it is, they will do these things, they will do these things. Goodbye, my dear fellow, goodbye, bye, bye.'

Roger went back to the pupils' room, very pleased with life. But, easy though his task was going to be, he wouldn't leave anything to chance. First he would master the facts, then the law and then – then – glorious moment – he would have a conference with his client.

'Hear you've got an undefended,' said Peter. 'I think they're a bore.'

'Have you done one?' asked Charles.

'No, but I've heard hundreds. Simple as pie – but an awful bore. No, give me something a bit meatier for my first brief.'

'Haven't you had one, then?' said Roger.

'As a matter of fact,' said Peter, 'it's not a terribly good thing to have a brief too early in one's career. Might come an awful cropper. Of course an undefended's different. But I just don't care for the sound of them. Shouldn't want my friends to send me one of those. If that's all the use they've got for me I'd rather they went somewhere else.'

' "Said the fox," ' said Charles, ' "adding to his wife, 'they always give me indigestion, anyway.' " '

'I don't know what you're talking about,' said Peter. 'Anyway I can't afford to waste my time here. I'm going down to the Bailey.'

'Hope you get that dock brief,' said Charles. 'That'll be a start.'

'Well done,' said Charles when Peter had left. 'Who sent it you?'

'Uncle of a girlfriend.'

'Good show. I never seem to be lucky that way. Are you going to have a conference?'

'I suppose so. It's marked on the brief – two guineas.'

'That doesn't mean a thing, as a matter of fact. They pay it whether you have one or not.'

'How odd,' said Roger.

'I suppose it's the same with every job. There are always things which are difficult to explain to people who aren't in it.'

'I suppose there are. But I think I ought to have a conference, anyway.'

'Is it sticky then?'

'Oh, I don't think so. I spoke to Grimes and he said it was all right. But I think I ought to ask her a few questions.'

'When'll you have it?'

'I don't know. What ought I to do about it? Speak to Alec?'

'Yes, I should think so. I've never had one yet.'

'You've never had a conference?'

'No, as I told you, we haven't all got girlfriends with solicitor uncles.'

'I am lucky.'

'I should say you are. That'll make up for what happened on your first day. Very different going into a

Court knowing all about it – with your own case too. What's it about?'

Roger told him and then went to arrange with Alec for a conference.

'You usually see them outside the Court, sir,' said Alec, 'but I can get them down here if you'd like.'

'Yes, I think so, please,' said Roger feeling very daring at giving orders to his clerk. Outside the Court did not seem to be the real thing.

After that he went to the Bar Library and read the case of *Herod v Herod* and several other later cases in which it had been approved. It seemed clear enough. Then he looked up every other point of law he could think of. He went back to chambers with a note of what he had read. Then he went home.

His mother was out. So he went straight to the telephone to thank Joy. 'It's terribly good of your uncle, Joy.'

'He's a dear old boy and if I give him a nice kiss, he'll do quite a lot for me. Shall I give him lots more kisses, Roger?'

'Oh, please, Joy.'

'What'll you give me then?'

'We'll go and dine.'

'Lovely. Where? When?'

'Well, I haven't had the cheque yet. I wonder when they send it.'

'I'd better give him another kiss, don't you think? I like talking about kisses to you, Roger. Don't you?'

'Of course I do, Joy, it is sweet of you. I can't thank you enough.'

'Oh, yes, you can. And I'll expect you to try.'

'Of course I will.'

'Promise.'

'Of course.'

'Roger, darling – how lovely. I'll go and see uncle tonight and we'll dine tomorrow. I'll lend you the money if the cheque hasn't come.'

'Oh – I couldn't let you. But I can try mother.'

As soon as he'd finished talking to Joy, blushing slightly he telephoned Sally.

'Oh, Roger, I am glad. What's it about?'

'Well, I'd rather like to talk to you about it, if I might. It's not the sort of thing I can mention on the telephone.'

'Well, when would you like?'

'You couldn't come round now? I expect mother's got enough food.'

'I'd love it.'

As soon as Sally had arrived Roger showed her the lovely brief, but he covered up the names with his hand.

'You can't possibly know the people in this case and it must be all right for me to tell you if you don't know their names. Even they wouldn't mean anything to you.'

'All right,' said Sally, 'if you say so.'

'D'you mind if I tell you about the case as though I were addressing the judge?' he asked.

'Of course not.'

'May it please your Lordship,' began Roger, 'my client who is a lady of mature years – '

'Stop,' said Sally, 'that won't do. How old is she?'

'Forty-five.'

'Well – she'd hit you over the head with her umbrella for that – out of Court if not in. Why mention her age, anyway?'

'I think it's important in this case. You see, Sally, there are things in this case which you and I wouldn't talk about normally – I mean – I know everyone does nowadays, but you're different. I do want you to understand that when I

82

talk about – talk about this woman's – this woman's – er – behaviour – it's only because it's in the case.'

'Strictly professionally,' said Sally. 'I suppose you're trying to tell me she's committed adultery.'

'Yes,' said Roger, 'I am, Sally, I'm afraid.'

'That's all right, Roger, it's not your fault; she did it, not you.'

'Quite,' said Roger. 'I'm so glad you understand. Now may I go on?'

'Please.'

'May it please your Lordship, my client who is no longer young – '

'No,' said Sally, 'if you must say anything about it, and I can't yet see why you should, say what her age is. She may not like that, but she'd prefer it to any of your phrases.'

'Oh, all right. My client who is forty-five is bringing this petition on the grounds of desertion. As your Lordship probably knows desertion is a matrimonial offence and consists of – '

'Just a moment, Roger,' interrupted Sally, 'I don't know anything about Courts and judges, but I suppose there have been a good many cases of desertion before yours.'

'Oh, Lord, yes.'

'Well – don't you think the judge might know what is meant by it then?'

'I said "as your Lordship probably knows – " '

'D'you think he'd like the "probably?" Some judges are pretty touchy, I believe.'

'All right then. As your Lordship knows – '

'Well, if he knows, why tell him?' said Sally.

'I'm sure I've read that they say things like that, Sally.'

'I expect that's when the judge *doesn't* know, Roger, and it's a polite way of telling him. If it's something that he must know and you know he must know it seems a bit odd to me telling him at all. You might just as well tell him that the case is brought under English law. I suppose every case is, unless it's a special one.'

'I say, you know, Sally, I do think you're marvellous. You ought to have gone to the Bar. You're going to be the most awful help to me. Oh – I could kiss you.'

Sally said nothing. Roger did nothing.

'Just another of your phrases, I suppose. Well, it's better than saying I'm of mature years. Though I expect I shall be before – now where were we?' she went on hurriedly.

'How would *you* start, Sally?'

'Well, I suppose, I'd say that it was a petition for divorce on the ground of desertion and then say shortly what the facts were.'

'When would you mention the discretion?'

'What discretion?'

Roger explained what was meant by a discretion statement and told Sally what was in it.

'But I don't understand,' said Sally.

'But I thought I'd made it clear. Where a petitioner has committed adultery he or she has got to file – '

'Oh, no, I understand all that. What I don't understand is what the husband has done wrong.'

'He left her and wouldn't come back.'

'Yes, but she'd committed adultery.'

'But he didn't know of it. It's all quite clear. It's in *Herod and Herod*. I read it this afternoon.'

'Are you sure you didn't misread it, Roger dear? After all you are fairly new to the game and I expect some of these things are difficult to understand – '

'Now, look, Sally. I think you're awfully clever and all that, and you're going to be an awful lot of use to me, if you will, but when I say the law's so and so you've got to accept it from me. I've looked it up.'

'But Roger, I'm sorry to seem so dense. Do try and make me understand it. I gather the law disapproves of adultery.'

'Of course.'

'I suppose the law agrees that it's a breach of the marriage vows or whatever the law calls them to commit adultery?'

'Certainly.'

'So if a wife commits adultery the husband is entitled to leave her.'

'Quite.'

'Well, that's what happened in your case.'

'He didn't know.'

'But surely, Roger, that can't make any difference.'

'Well, it does.'

'I still can't believe it,' said Sally. 'Look. Marriage starts with a husband and wife living together, doesn't it?'

'Yes.'

'And if one leaves the other it's desertion.'

'Exactly. That's what's happened here. He's left her.'

'Not so fast, Roger. Is a wife entitled to have her husband living with her if she commits adultery?'

'No,' began Roger – and then seeing where this admission was leading him to, he went on: 'Well, it depends. If the husband finds out he can leave her.'

'And are you really saying that if the husband doesn't find out – if the lady's clever enough to conceal it from him – then she has the right that he should go on living with her?'

'That,' said Roger, 'is the law of England.'

'I'm sorry,' said Sally, 'you know and I don't. You've just looked it up. You've taken all your Bar examinations. But I just can't believe it. You're saying that, provided a man or woman is a good enough liar, he or she can commit adultery as much as they like?'

'It sounds odd put that way, I agree,' said Roger.

'Well, isn't that what you were saying?'

Roger thought for a moment.

'I suppose it is really. I must say it does sound strange the way you put it. I didn't think of it like that, and I'm sure there's nothing in the cases I looked at about it. I think I'd better look at them again. I say, Sally, you really are a wonder. I could – didn't I hear mother?'

'You should know by now, Roger,' said Sally.

'Oh, no, it's the people next door.'

'Yes, Roger. You were saying?'

'Where was I now? Oh, yes – well, when do you think I should mention this discretion business?'

'Wouldn't it be a good thing to go and hear one or two undefended divorces yourself first, so that you can see when it's normally done?'

'How right you are. I will.'

'May I come and hear you do yours, Roger?'

'Of course – that is – well – '

'Well, of course, if I'll make you nervous, Roger – '

'It's not exactly that, Sally. You see – as a matter of fact – it's like this really – of course I'd love you to be there – but, as a matter of fact, well – Joy's uncle sent me the brief actually.'

'Well,' said Sally, 'that was very nice of him – and her, but why should that make any difference? Or have they taken the whole Court for the occasion?'

'No, of course not, but I expect Joy would like to be there – and I thought, I mean, mightn't it be a bit embarrassing? For both of you, I mean. And as it was Joy's uncle who sent the brief – '

'And Joy who helped you to prepare it?'

'That isn't fair, Sally. I won't ask you another time if you're going to throw it in my teeth.'

'I simply asked if I could come to hear you. I'm not throwing anything in your teeth. Joy and I won't tear each other's eyes out, you know. We'd be sent to prison if we did. Which of us would you defend, Roger, if we were? You couldn't do both, could you?'

'I think that's a horrible question,' said Roger.

CHAPTER EIGHT

First Conference

Two days later Roger had his first conference. Peter and Charles went into Henry's room so that he could have the pupils' room for the purpose.

Mrs Newent came with Mr Smith, a managing clerk from Messrs Thornton, Merivale & Co, who introduced himself and his client to Roger. He invited them to sit down. They did so. Mrs Newent was attractive in a cheap sort of way, rather overdressed and too much made-up. She had very shapely legs with sheer nylon stockings and she showed Roger much too much of them both. His eyes followed their movements, which were fairly frequent, as a rabbit's eyes follow a snake. From time to time with an effort he would look at the ceiling or out of the window or at the bookshelves, but it was no use. Back they had to come. He had never been so close to such things before. They revolted but fascinated him, and he simply could not help himself. He cleared his throat preparatorily to opening the proceedings. But Mrs Newent got in first.

'You're very young, if I may say so,' she said. She did not mean that she was in the least dismayed. Several of her friends had had divorces. One had to go through the formalities and that was all. Indeed, it was very nice to be represented by a pleasant-looking young man who couldn't keep his eyes off one's legs.

'It must be an awful responsibility,' she added.

Roger coughed. 'That's what we're here for,' he said eventually.

'I'm so glad,' said Mrs Newent, and recrossed her legs. 'I feel sort of safe with you.'

Even at that early stage and even with his inexperience, Roger began to wonder whether the discretion statement constituted the full and frank disclosure which such statements are supposed to be. He remembered, too, that the statement said quite a number of things about the husband and the dance and so forth, but when it came to the adultery it was disposed of in a very few words. The reason for Mr Storrington going into her bedroom was slurred over in the words, 'Somehow or other he came in.'

'Now,' went on Mrs Newent, 'was there something you wanted to ask me?'

By this time Roger had looked again at the cases and it certainly seemed as if what he had told Sally was right. It appeared that, in spite of Sally's doubts, the law was that, provided the adulteress was clever enough, she had the right that her husband should go on living with her. But there was just the point that it was for her to prove that her husband knew nothing about it. Roger quite rightly wanted to be sure of this.

'It's about your discretion statement,' he began.

'Mr Smith here wrote that out,' said Mrs Newent. 'I only signed it, you know. That's right, isn't it, Mr Smith?'

'I wrote it out on your instructions, Mrs Newent.'

'Instructions? I don't remember giving any instructions.'

'It's what you told me, I mean.'

'Oh, yes. What long words you lawyers use. If you'd said that at first I'd have understood.'

'I take it the statement is true, Mrs Newent?' asked Roger.

'True?' said Mrs Newent, recrossing her legs. 'Of course. Mr Smith wouldn't have written it down otherwise, would he?'

'There was only the once and you'd had a little too much to drink.'

'That's right. Gin and frenches all the evening. I felt on top of the world.'

'I thought you became dizzy and faint.'

'That's right.'

'After you felt on top of the world you became dizzy and faint?' asked Roger.

'That's right,' said Mrs Newent. 'You are a clever young man. I'm glad I've got you. D'you mind if I have a cigarette?'

'Of course not,' said Roger and offered her one and lit it for her. She guided his hand to the cigarette, much to his discomfort.

'I think you ought to do very well,' she said. 'I shall remember you appeared for me when I see your name in the papers.'

Roger blushed and coughed and tried to look at the ceiling.

'Now, there's another thing,' he said. 'Are you quite sure that your husband knew nothing about this and suspected nothing?' For answer Mrs Newent put her first finger to the side of her nose and winked.

'Are you sure?' repeated Roger.

'Not a notion,' said Mrs Newent. 'We were discretion itself, if you'll pardon my using the word.'

'But,' said Roger, 'it only happened once and then you were faint and dizzy. How can you have been discretion itself if you were faint and dizzy?'

'Come now, young man,' said Mrs Newent. 'I'm not sure you're as clever as I thought. I go to a dance. Right?'

'Yes,' said Roger.

'I drink too much. Right?'

'Yes,' said Roger.

'I go out into the cold air and as every judge knows – I should hope – it hits me for six. Right?'

'You became faint and dizzy.'

'Exactly. So he helps me home. Now I'm home. I'm still faint and dizzy at the bottom of the stairs. Can't get up by myself. Right?'

'Yes.'

'He helps me up the stairs. We get to my room. Still faint and dizzy. With me?'

'Yes.'

'Like the perfect gentleman he is he sees me into my bedroom. All clear so far?'

'Yes.'

'Right. Well, when we get into the bedroom we take a liking to each other – see, and I become less faint and dizzy. But it was too late then.'

'How do you know your husband knows nothing about it?'

'Because he wasn't there and no one could have told him. As soon as we took a liking to one another I sent Bert out of the room to his own room, making enough noise that people in the next room would have heard him go away within a minute or two of his coming in. Then he comes back like a mouse. Didn't even hear him come in myself. Didn't hear him go, either. I was asleep then. But I know he was ever so careful.'

'When your husband came back, did he seem to suspect anything?'

'Not a thing. He was just the same as ever. Cold as an iceberg. A woman's got to get a bit of warmth from someone, hasn't she?'

'But it was only once?'

'It was only once,' replied Mrs Newent with emphasis. 'Because I know what's nice,' she added, 'that doesn't mean to say I don't know what's wrong. And with all the other boarders around you've got to be careful. People talk. Now what else d'you want to ask me? I'm getting a bit tired of this cross-questioning. I thought you were on my side.'

'Of course I'm on your side,' said Roger, 'but I have to ask you these questions.'

'Well, I can't think why,' said Mrs Newent. 'It's all plain and straightforward. I want a divorce, Mr Newent wants a divorce, what more d'you want? I don't know why there's all this palaver, anyway.'

'We don't have divorce by consent in this country,' said Roger.

'Well – who says it's by consent? He left me, didn't he? That's desertion, isn't it? Then you have this ridiculous business about discretion. I wouldn't have told you if I'd known there'd be all this fuss. Was I faint and dizzy? When did I stop being faint and dizzy? And if not, why not? You wouldn't have known if I hadn't told you and there wouldn't have been all this nonsense. I'll know better another time. I thought one could trust one's lawyer.'

'We have a duty to the Court,' said Mr Smith.

'Fiddlesticks,' said Mrs Newent. 'A lot of old fools sitting up there, what do they care? They're half asleep, anyway. I went with my friend the other day. No fuss about hers. All over in five minutes. She didn't put in any discretion statement either, not on your sweet life. She couldn't have remembered for one thing. I'm too honest, that's my trouble. And what do I get for it? Asked a lot of intimate questions. I'd be ashamed if I were a man. It's not as though I'd done anything really wrong.'

'But I thought you said – ' began Roger.

'All right, Mr Clever, not as wrong as all that. There are worse things. Murder, for instance, or blackmail. All right, I was wrong to let him in my room that night. All right. I've told you. There it is in black and white. You've got my ruddy discretion statement and I hope it chokes you both – and the judge. Now, is there anything else you want?'

The conference was very different from the one Roger had visualized and he was glad when it ended. He felt slightly sick. Mrs Newent was not quite the sort of maiden he would care to rescue, even fully clothed.

CHAPTER NINE

Joyce

That evening he dined with Joy. He had not had the cheque from the solicitors, but his mother had lent him the money.

'Of course, darling,' she had said. 'It'll be an investment, really. You'll be able to keep me soon. Won't that be lovely? And I shan't have to look to Aunt Ethel for a new dress. I do think you're clever, darling.'

'It was Joy really, Mother.'

'But I'm sure the solicitors wouldn't have sent it to you if they hadn't heard of your reputation. I shall tell everyone about you. Fancy making a name for yourself in a week. But then I knew you would. It's your father in you. Not me, I'm afraid. Now that it's all right, I don't mind telling you, I've always been a little frightened that you might be a fool like me. I'm so glad you're not, darling. Shall we get a bottle of champagne and celebrate. We can pay for it next month.'

'That'd be lovely, darling, but I must go out with Joy tonight.'

'Oh, of course.'

'And you mustn't start talking about my having made a name for myself. I haven't done anything of the sort. I've been sent my first brief by the uncle of a girlfriend and it's just an undefended divorce. I haven't even done it yet. I might make an awful mess of it.'

'Oh, no you won't, not you.'

'Well, I hope not, but – oh, darling, I'm appearing for the most awful woman. I'm so glad you're not like her.'

'Thank you, darling. So am I, if she's all that awful.'

'She's really terrible. It makes me feel uncomfortable to meet her. And the things she says. D'you know I felt quite sick after I'd had a conference with her. Don't tell anyone else. I suppose one's got to get used to that sort of thing, but I hope I don't get many more like her. I'll be glad when it's over. Would you like to come and hear it?'

'Darling, of course. When is it?'

'Tomorrow.'

'You must tell me how to get there. Or will you take me?'

'Well, darling – you know I'd love to take you – but don't you think it would look a bit obvious if we went in together? Rather like showing off. Besides, I don't want it to look as if it were my first brief. You do understand, don't you?'

'Of course, darling. I won't come at all, if you'd rather not.'

'No, I'd love you to.'

'I shan't make you nervous?'

'Oh, no – once it's started, I shall be all right.'

'Well, you must tell me where it is. One of those places with blue lamps outside them, is it?'

'Mother, darling, those are police stations.'

'That's right. Well, there's a Court next to them sometimes, isn't there?'

'Mother, this is the High Court of Justice, Probate, Divorce and Admiralty Division. It's in the Law Courts in the Strand. It's the most important legal place there is, except the House of Lords and Privy Council.'

'Well, you mustn't be cross with me, darling. I don't know anything about the law. And what did you say about Admiralty? I thought yours was a divorce case. Does an admiral try it? I must say, he'd look rather sweet with his cocked hat.'

'No, it's the Divorce Division, but that's linked up with Admiralty and Probate for historical reasons. But it won't be an admiral in a cocked hat. It'll be a judge in a wig and gown. And I'll be in mine too. I'll tell you how to get there and which Court it's in. Now I really must fly or I'll be late for Joy. Thank you so much for the money.'

Joy was all ready for him, looking very pretty indeed. They went to a Soho restaurant.

'This is going to be a lovely evening,' said Joy on the way. 'I'm so proud of you, Roger. I know you're going to do terribly well. Uncle Alfred's very impressed too. He says there's an awful shortage of young men at the Bar and you're just what he's looking for. You mustn't say I told you, but if you do this case all right, he's going to send you a lot more.'

'Oh – Joy, it sounds too good to be true.'

'I gave him such a nice kiss for it. Right in the middle of his forehead. Funny, that's where he likes it. It's not my idea. But then an uncle's different. Oh, here we are. It's going to be a lovely evening, Roger.'

She squeezed his arm.

'Two, sir?' said the waiter. 'Over here, sir, if you please. Will this suit you, sir? Thank you, sir. And what about a little aperitif before dinner? Dry Martini, glass of sherry, anything you like, sir?'

'Do you think I should, Joy? I shall want a clear head in the morning.'

'Of course, silly. It won't hurt you at all. Buck you up. Stop you feeling nervous. I'll have a Dry Martini, please. You do the same, Roger. It'll be good for you.'

So they each had a Dry Martini and with their dinner they had a bottle of wine and by the middle of dinner, Roger, egged on by Joy, could see himself persuading judges, convincing juries and generally making a big name for himself at the Bar.

'Then you'll become a QC, Roger. I'm sure you'll be the youngest ever.'

'D'you really think so?'

'Of course I do. But then I expect you'll forget all about little me.'

'How can you say such a thing? It'll all be due to you really.'

'Then you won't drop me like an old sock when you're successful?'

'I'm not like that, Joy.'

'No, Roger, but you'll have so many people around you. I'm not very big, Roger. Sally's much taller.'

'Don't let's talk about Sally.'

Even older men can imagine a lot and forget a lot under the influence of a few drinks. At twenty-one all sorts of things can happen. To Roger, Joy seemed prettier than she'd ever been, really lovely, so that when she eventually said softly, looking down at her coffee: 'Roger, will you be a little loving to me tonight?' he was able to answer without any effort: 'Joy, darling, you know I will.'

'Roger, darling.'

Everything felt strangely unreal to Roger and it was very pleasant. He was going to be a great man and he had the prettiest girl in the world opposite him. Life was very good, very good indeed. Then he thought of his case in the morning. Perhaps it would be reported in the papers. Oh, no, of course it couldn't be, except for the judge's judgment. Thinking of the case he suddenly thought of his client, Mrs Newent. It gave him a slightly unpleasant shock but, when he mentioned her, Joy helped him by saying: 'But in a great career you're bound to come across nasty people. Someone had to defend Crippen, didn't they?'

'Of course. How silly of me.'

They got up from the table. Roger felt slightly wobbly on his feet. Suddenly he thought of his client again. 'Faint and dizzy.' Well, he didn't feel faint or dizzy, but he did feel as though everything was very easy to do. A lack of restraint, that's what it was. Had he misjudged Mrs Newent? Perhaps she wasn't used to drink and it had done something to her. He could understand it now. He had never really wanted to kiss Joy before. But when she put herself in his arms in the taxi, there was no difficulty about it at all.

'Darling, you're wonderful,' he said.

'Roger, I love you.'

'I love you, Joy.'

'Oh, Roger, I'm so happy.'

CHAPTER TEN

The Divorce Court

The next morning Roger woke with a slight headache. There was a ring on the telephone. He got out of bed and answered it. It was Sally.

'Just to wish you good luck, Roger. I shall be there, but you needn't take any notice of me.'

'Oh, thank you, Sally. Thank you very much for ringing.'

He went back to bed for a few minutes. What had he said to Joy the night before? What hadn't he said? Oh, dear, how difficult it all was. And they'd both be there. Well, he mustn't think of that now. He must concentrate on his case. He had found out that you don't normally address the judge in an undefended divorce case before calling your evidence. Henry had told him and he'd been to hear some cases, as Sally had suggested. They certainly sounded simple enough.

He got to chambers early and found Henry there already.

'Who are you in front of?' Henry asked.

'Judge Crane.'

'Oh, that's good. You'll be all right in front of him. Bit of luck for you you're not before Judge Ryman. He's sitting today. He can be very difficult. He actually tries all his cases. It can be very awkward. Personally, I think he's right, but I'm in a decided minority. I think it's for Parliament to change the law if people want divorce made easier. But very few people agree with me. I expect I'm wrong, but there it is. Glad you're not in front of Ryman. That would have been a bit tough for your first case.'

At ten minutes past ten Roger, feeling rather self-conscious, walked across the Strand carrying his blue bag. He was on the way to the robing-room. At the entrance to the Law Courts he met his mother.

'Not late, you see, darling,' she said. 'Can you tell me where I go?'

'Would you mind very much asking an attendant? I've got to go and robe and I don't want to be late. We're sixth in the list, but you can never tell. Some of the people in the first five cases might not be there.'

He felt a little like he did in his first days at a public school when he was terrified his mother would call him by his Christian name.

He robed and went to the Court. He found Mrs Newent outside. She did not at first recognize him in his wig. She had recovered from her fit of anger in chambers and, feeling a little nervous herself, wanted someone to be nice to her.

'You look sweet,' she said.

Roger blushed and coughed.

'I don't think we'll have to wait very long,' he said.

'It's going to be all right, isn't it?' said Mrs Newent.

'Oh, yes, I think so,' said Roger with reasonable confidence. Now that it was so near to the beginning of the battle, he was glad to think that Judge Crane was an easy judge. How nice of Henry to tell him. What a good chap he was. It made all the difference. He did in fact feel a little weak at the knees. He walked into the Court and at once saw Joy sitting at one end and Sally at the other. They were both attractively dressed. He tried not to let them see he had noticed them. His mother was sitting in the middle of a row. Counsel's row was almost full, but he was just able to get a seat at the end. A few minutes later the judge came in. The associate got up and called: 'Foster against Foster,' and then handed the papers in the case to the judge. Counsel got up and the case began.

'May it please your Lordship, this is a husband's petition on the grounds of desertion. Mr Foster, please.'

A man went into the witness box and took the oath. The following dialogue took place:

COUNSEL: 'Is your full name Ernest Edward Foster?'

THE WITNESS: 'Yes.'

COUNSEL: 'Where do you now live, Mr Foster?'

THE WITNESS: 'Apple Tree Lodge, Buckley, Essex.'

COUNSEL: 'And were you married on the 14th day of June 1930 to Elizabeth Foster, whose maiden name was Hadlow at the Register Office for the District of Bilcombe in the County of Surrey?'

THE WITNESS: 'Yes.'

COUNSEL: 'And there are no children of the marriage?'

THE WITNESS: 'No.'

COUNSEL: 'And after the marriage did you live at various places with your wife and finally at Apple Tree Lodge where you now are?'

THE WITNESS: 'Yes.'

COUNSEL: 'Now I think your marriage was quite happy at first, but after that did relations between you and your wife become strained?'

THE WITNESS: 'Yes.'

COUNSEL: 'And were there disagreements and quarrels and so forth?'

THE WITNESS: 'Yes.'

COUNSEL: 'And finally on the 14th June 1946 did she leave you?'

THE WITNESS: 'Yes.'

COUNSEL: 'Did she say anything before she left?'

THE WITNESS: 'No.'

COUNSEL: 'Nothing at all?'

THE WITNESS: 'No.'

COUNSEL: 'Didn't she say anything about never coming back to you again?'

JUDGE CRANE: 'I think that's a little leading, Mr Fox.'

COUNSEL: 'I'm sorry, my Lord. Did she or did she not say anything about not coming back to you again?'

THE WITNESS: 'She did.'

COUNSEL: 'What did she say?'

THE WITNESS: 'That she wouldn't come back.'

COUNSEL: 'And has she ever come back?'

THE WITNESS: 'No.'

COUNSEL: 'Now, will you look at these two letters. There are copies for my Lord. (*Letters handed to Witness.*) Are those letters in your wife's handwriting?'

THE WITNESS: 'Yes.'

COUNSEL: 'Your Lordship will see that in them she repeats that she will never come back to the petitioner again.'

JUDGE CRANE: 'Yes, I see.'

COUNSEL: 'Now may he see the acknowledgment of service? (*Document handed to the Witness.*) Do you see a signature you recognize at the bottom of that document?'

THE WITNESS: 'Yes.'

COUNSEL: 'Whose is it?'

THE WITNESS: 'My wife's.'

COUNSEL: 'Thank you, Mr Foster. My Lord, if your Lordship is satisfied on the evidence I ask for a decree nisi.'

JUDGE CRANE: 'Very well, Mr Fox. Decree nisi.'

The next case was called. The dialogue was very much the same, except that that case was, like Roger's, a discretion case. The petitioner was a man and, in addition to evidence very similar to that which had been given in the last case, the following passage occurred:

COUNSEL: 'May the witness see his discretion statement? (*The document is shown to the Witness.*) Now, Mr Brown, do you see a signature at the bottom of that document which you recognize?'

THE WITNESS: 'Yes.'

COUNSEL: 'Whose is it?'

THE WITNESS: 'Mine.'

COUNSEL: 'Before you signed that document, did you read it through carefully?'

THE WITNESS: 'I did.'

COUNSEL: 'Are the contents true?'

THE WITNESS: 'They are.'

COUNSEL: 'And have you committed adultery with anyone else or on any other occasions than are mentioned in that statement?'

THE WITNESS: 'No.'

COUNSEL: 'Thank you, Mr Brown. My Lord, upon that evidence, I respectfully submit that this is a case in which your Lordship can properly exercise your discretion in favour of the petitioner and if your Lordship is satisfied, I ask you to do so and to pronounce a decree nisi.'

JUDGE CRANE: 'Very well. I exercise my discretion in favour of the petitioner and grant a decree nisi.'

It was all very short, thought Roger. He would like, if he could, to make rather more of his case, if possible. He didn't want trouble, but this was, if anything, too easy. Mrs Newent, on the other hand, was very satisfied. This, she told herself, was exactly and precisely what the doctor had ordered. Her confidence now almost completely restored, she began to wonder where she and Mr Storrington should go and have a celebration that night. Just at that moment another associate came in and spoke to his colleague sitting below Judge Crane.

The latter, after a whispered conversation with him, stood up and spoke to the judge in an undertone. Then he announced: 'The following cases will be taken before His Honour Judge Ryman in Probate Divorce and Admiralty Court 4. Will the parties and their witnesses please proceed to that Court at once. Speed and Speed, Newent and Newent, Layer and Layer.'

As Roger got up to go counsel next to him said: 'Bad luck, old boy. Glad it isn't me.'

Roger felt his inside leave him for the floor. Why had he said to himself that he'd like to make a little more of his case? This was fate's revenge. He wondered what Ryman was like. Oh, well, there was nothing for it. And anyway he would see him try one case first, that was something. Fortunately Mrs Newent was quite unaware that there had been any change in her fortunes. She assumed that much the same happened in every Court. Roger started on his way to Court 4, with the managing clerk from her solicitors, and followed by Mrs Newent, his mother, Joy and Sally, who walked along together.

'So glad you could come,' said Joy.

'I'd have hated to disappoint you,' said Sally.

Roger went into the Court where Judge Ryman was sitting. After a short delay the associate called: 'Speed against Speed.'

Counsel next to Roger stood up and put his client, a woman, into the witness box. Roger looked at the judge. He noticed nothing particularly forbidding about his appearance and was grateful for that. Mrs Speed was petitioning for a divorce on the ground of cruelty. After counsel had asked the preliminary questions about the marriage, he started to ask about the history of the married life.

'Did he ever hit you?' he asked.

'Really,' said the judge, 'the Court of Appeal and the learned President have said more than once that leading questions should not be asked. This is a petition on the ground of cruelty. Please don't lead on any essential matters.'

'If your Lordship pleases. Well, Mrs Speed, did he or did he not hit you?'

'Really,' said the judge, 'that's just as bad.'

'With great respect, my Lord,' said counsel, who was a fierce little man with more ferocity than sense or knowledge. 'That was not a leading question. She could have said "yes" or "no." '

'I'm sorry to disagree, Mr Brunt,' said the judge. 'The witness could have answered "yes" or "no" to your first question, but it was none the less leading. So is this one.'

'Well, my Lord, I've often asked this kind of question at the Old Bailey without objection.'

'I'm afraid I'm only concerned with this Court, Mr Brunt.'

'My Lord, I wish to be heard on this point.'

'By all means, Mr Brunt, if you think it of any value. You can always go to the Court of Appeal, you know, if you object to my ruling.'

'Think of the expense, my Lord. My client wants a divorce, not a visit to all the Courts in the country.'

'Please behave yourself Mr Brunt. I can only say that if your client wants a divorce she must give her evidence without the assistance of leading questions. That is particularly the case in a matter such as the present one where, no doubt, the bulk of the evidence will be that of your client herself. I have to make up my mind whether I believe her or not. That's difficult enough anyway in most undefended cases. It's impossible if she only answers "yes" or "no." '

'Very well, my Lord. I have made my protest,' said Mr Brunt.

'Now, Mrs Speed, how often did these assaults take place?'

'Mr Brunt,' said the judge, 'I'm sorry to have to interrupt you again so soon, but that is not only a leading question, it is a double question and a most improper one in view of my ruling. The witness has not yet said that her husband did hit her.'

'Well, madam,' said Mr Brunt in a voice in which he did not conceal the annoyance, 'did he hit you?'

'Really, Mr Brunt,' said the judge. 'There must be a limit to all this.'

'Really, my Lord,' said Mr Brunt angrily. 'Your Lordship told me to ask the question and then your Lordship complains when I do ask it. I agree that there must be a limit.'

'Mr Brunt, that was a most improper observation. I must ask you to apologize for it.'

Mr Brunt hesitated, made a quick appreciation, decided he had gone too far, though in his view not without extreme provocation, and said: 'I apologize, my Lord, but it is very difficult to know what questions to ask in front of your Lordship.'

'Well, please try, Mr Brunt,' said the judge. 'Only don't make them leading questions. If you would like me to suggest one, I will.'

'That would be most kind of your Lordship.'

'Perhaps you'd better ask her how her husband treated her after the first few months of married life.'

'Thank you, my Lord, I will.'

Meantime, Roger, who was not altogether able to make up his mind whether Mr Brunt or the judge was in the right, realized that what Henry had said had been only too true. He prayed that he would be able to avoid leading questions. It's very difficult if you don't really know what they are. Roger did not yet appreciate that the context or circumstances in which a question is asked may make it leading and that the question, 'Did he or did he not do so-and-so' may, according to the circumstances, be a grossly leading question or not a leading question at all.

'He treated me like a slave,' said the witness.

'In what way?' asked Mr Brunt.

'In every way.'

'Would you be a little more explicit, please madam,' said Mr Brunt. 'Enumerate some of the ways.'

'En – enu – enum – ?' said the witness, puzzled.

'Give some examples,' paraphrased Mr Brunt.

'It was always happening.'

'What was always happening, Mrs Speed?' asked the judge.

'Him treating me like that, your Honour.'

'Yes, but how did he treat you?' asked the judge.

'Oh, terrible.'

'Yes, but we weren't there, Mrs Speed. You must tell us what he did,' said the judge.

'It was all the time.'

'But what was all the time?' said the judge.

'What he did.'

'But what was it?' said the judge.

'Everything.'

'Tell me one thing he did,' said the judge.

'There were so many.'

'Then it should be easy to tell me one,' said the judge.

'It's a long time ago.'

'Well, Mr Brunt, you must see if you can elicit anything from the witness. I've tried, but with no success, I'm afraid,' said the judge.

'Madam,' said Mr Brunt, 'what did your husband do to you?'

'It was that time at Christmas,' said Mrs Speed.

'What happened at Christmas?' said Mr Brunt.

'No, it was Easter,' said Mrs Speed. 'You've got me all flummoxed.'

'Well, what happened at Easter?' asked Mr Brunt.

'You want me to tell the judge?'

'That's what I've been asking you to do for the last five minutes,' said Mr Brunt.

'I didn't half tell him off,' said Mrs Speed, 'but I don't think he heard me.'

'How long was this case supposed to take?' asked the judge.

'Fifteen minutes, my Lord,' said the associate.

'Well, it's taken nearly that to get this witness' name and address, which is about all we have got so far. Mr Brunt, would you like me to stand the case over to be started afresh another day before another judge? At this rate it will need at least an hour.'

'If your Lordship had let me ask the questions as I wanted to,' said Mr Brunt, 'it might have been over by now.'

'Equally,' said the judge, 'if I'd let you give the evidence. I thought possibly, Mr Brunt, you'd *like* the case to be stood over and heard *de novo* by another judge.'

'Yes,' said Mr Brunt, 'I think perhaps I'll accept your Lordship's kind suggestions.'

The case was accordingly adjourned and Roger, now on the high diving-board, waited for the word to go.

'Newent against Newent,' called the associate.

'May it please your Lordship, this is a wife's petition on the ground of desertion. I should tell your Lordship that it's a discretion case. Mrs Newent, please.'

'Are you putting in the discretion statement now, Mr Thursby?' asked the judge.

Do I or don't I, thought Roger. I don't know. Why hadn't I asked? Here I am, stuck before I started and mother's here and Joy and Sally. Oh, hell, why didn't I watch what they usually do?

The judge noticed the pause and Roger's white wig and said pleasantly: 'That's the usual course, Mr Thursby, unless there's some special reason for not doing so.'

'Very well, my Lord,' said Roger gratefully. 'I'll put it in now.'

'Very well, Mr Thursby, thank you,' said the judge.

That was better. It was good to be called Mr Thursby and now he was on an even keel again.

Mrs Newent was sworn and was asked by Roger the usual preliminary questions.

'And now, Mrs Newent, will you tell his Lordship how your married life went?' asked Roger.

'It was all right at first,' she said, 'but after that he started picking on me, said I paid more attention to my boarders than to him.'

'And did you?' intervened the judge.

'Not more than was necessary, my Lord. There's a lot of work to do running a boarding house.'

'Yes, Mr Thursby?' said the judge.

'And what happened in the end?' asked Roger.

'He left me,' said Mrs Newent.

It seemed very little to ask, thought Roger, but what more is there? Oh, yes, the letters.

'After he left you, did he write to you, or did you write to him?' asked Roger and then added, 'Or not,' in case it was a leading question.

The judge smiled.

'That wouldn't really cure it, Mr Thursby,' he said, 'if it needed a cure, but fortunately it didn't.'

'Thank you, my Lord,' said Roger.

'I wrote to him once or twice,' said Mrs Newent.

'What did you say in your letters?' asked Roger.

'Has notice to produce been given?' asked the judge.

'I don't know, my Lord,' said Roger.

'Well, perhaps you'd ask your client then.'

'Has notice to produce been given?' said Roger.

'Pardon?' said Mrs Newent.

'No, your solicitor client, Mr Thursby,' said the judge.

'I'm sorry, my Lord,' said Roger suddenly realizing what he'd done. He turned to Mr Smith and asked him if notice to produce had been given.

'Of course. It says so in the brief, doesn't it?' said Mr Smith. He was an experienced managing clerk and did not like what was happening.

'Yes, my Lord,' said Roger.

'Very well,' said the judge. 'You can ask what was in the letters.'

'What was in the letters?' asked Roger.

'I don't really remember,' said Mrs Newent.

'So much for them,' said the judge. 'But what about the letters from the husband? Were there any?'

'Yes, my Lord,' said Roger.

'Well, you can put those to her,' said the judge.

'Did you receive these letters from your husband, Mrs Newent?' asked Roger, and then started to open his mouth to say 'or not' and just checked himself in time. He must remember to ask Henry about leading questions.

'Yes,' said Mrs Newent, 'these are in his handwriting.'

The letters were handed to the judge and he read them.

'Yes, Mr Thursby?'

'Has he returned to you, Mrs Newent?'

'No.'

'Or offered to return?' asked the judge.

'No.'

'Or to make a home for you?'

'No.'

For some reason that he could never make out, Roger then proceeded to sit down, as though the case was over. The judge seemed to realize what had happened and quietly said: 'Discretion, Mr Thursby?'

Roger jumped up, blushing.

'I'm sorry, my Lord. Mrs Newent, would you look at your discretion statement.'

He asked her the necessary questions about the statement, ending with: 'Have you ever committed adultery except as stated in your statement?'

'No,' said Mrs Newent firmly.

'What else, if anything, has taken place between you and the man named in your statement?' asked the judge.

'What else?' repeated Mrs Newent, a little nervously.

The judge nodded.

'Nothing.'

'But you say you are living on affectionate terms in the same house. Has he suggested further acts of adultery to you?'

'No, my Lord.'

'Why not?'

Mrs Newent was totally at a loss to answer the question.

'You're living in the same house and you want to get married. Presumably you're still attracted to one another. You've committed adultery once, so neither of you have

111

any conscientious objection to doing so. I could understand your refusing, but I don't quite understand his not asking you.'

'Oh, I see what you mean, my Lord. Yes, he did ask me.'

'But you refused?'

'Yes.'

'Because you thought it wrong?'

'Yes, my Lord.'

'Thank you, Mrs Newent,' said the judge. 'There's only one other question I want to ask you. How long was it after your admitted act of adultery that your husband left you?'

'About a couple of months, my Lord.'

'Thank you, Mrs Newent,' said the judge.

Suddenly Roger thought he scented danger.

'Are you sure your husband never knew of your adultery, Mrs Newent?' he asked.

'Well,' said the judge, 'that is, I'm afraid, a leading question, but, now it's asked, she'd better answer it.'

'Quite sure,' said Mrs Newent firmly. 'He never knew or suspected a thing.'

'Did you treat your husband in exactly the same way, after your adultery with Mr Storrington, as before?'

'How d'you mean, my Lord, the same way?'

'Well, for instance, you say that you were ashamed the next morning. Your shame might have resulted in your treating your husband rather differently, don't you think?'

'I don't really know, my Lord.'

'You continued to share the same room?'

'The same room, my Lord, but not the same bed. We hadn't for some time.'

'Yes, Mr Thursby,' said the judge. 'Any further questions?'

Roger thought for a moment. He could not think of anything else to ask.

112

'No, thank you, my Lord,' he said. There was then a pause while Roger made up his mind what to do next. You ask for a decree, don't you, he said to himself. That's it, I think. Or is there anything else first? I'm not sure. Oh, well – 'Upon that evidence, my Lord – '

'Acknowledgment of service, Mr Thursby?'

'I'm sorry, my Lord.'

Of course, he would forget that. That made at least two things he'd forgotten, but thank Heaven the case was almost over. In a moment or so he would be outside the Court. It had been pretty bad, but it could have been worse. The witness identified her husband's signature on the document acknowledging receipt of the petition and then she left the witness box.

'Yes, Mr Thursby?' said the judge.

'Upon that evidence, my Lord, I ask your Lordship to exercise your discretion and grant a decree nisi with costs.'

There, he'd said it and his first case was about to be over.

Not much credit winning an undefended case, but still – what was that? What was the judge saying?

'It's not quite as simple as that, Mr Thursby.' What on earth was he talking about? Surely he knew about *Herod and Herod.*

'You see, Mr Thursby,' went on the judge, 'your client committed adultery before her husband left her.'

'Yes, my Lord,' began Roger with no clear realization of what he was going to say, 'but – but – ' very tentatively he started to say, 'Her – Herod – '

'But is it quite clear,' went on the judge, 'that *Herod and Herod* applies to a case where adultery is committed *before* the other spouse leaves? It strikes me as a bit odd that a wife who commits adultery should still have the right to the consortium of her husband, provided she's a good enough liar.'

Good Heavens, thought Roger, that's exactly what Sally said.

'How can you desert someone who hasn't the right to be lived with?' went on the judge.

'My Lord,' began Roger, but it was much too difficult. He wanted to say something about *Herod*'s case, but had no idea how to put it. As if reading his thoughts, the judge continued: 'I know there's a passage in *Herod* which helps you, but is it more than a dictum? We'd better look at it, hadn't we?'

The judge sent for that case and for some others. After reading several passages aloud and talking to Roger, who was almost unable to say anything except, 'Yes, my Lord,' or 'No, my Lord,' the judge eventually said: 'Well, Mr Thursby, much as I regret it, you have convinced me that the principle must be the same in each case, although with the greatest respect to the judges concerned, I cannot think that it is the law of this country that the adulterer who can lie well enough is entitled to the consortium of the other spouse, and that it is only the less efficient liar who loses the right to be lived with.'

Roger was now extremely pleased. The judge had said – quite untruthfully – that Roger had convinced him. They were words to be treasured. And so he'd won his case after all. And there *had* been a struggle, which made victory all the sweeter.

'Then, my Lord,' began Roger, 'I ask – '

'But I'm afraid,' went on the judge, 'that isn't the end of the matter. *Herod* and all the other cases make it quite plain that it is for the petitioner to prove that the adultery has not caused the desertion. That's so, is it not, Mr Thursby?'

'Yes, my Lord.'

'Well – have you proved it?'

'The evidence is, my Lord, that the husband did not know of it.'

'I agree that is the evidence and though I was not much impressed by your client, I'll assume for the moment that he didn't know. But is that enough?'

Roger was now completely out of his depth. There was nothing he could say.

'I don't know whether you're prepared to argue the point today,' said the judge. 'If not, I'll give you an adjournment to enable you to do so on a later occasion.'

'That's very good of your Lordship,' said Roger, having no idea what the point was.

'The point is this, Mr Thursby. I know that you can show me cases where it has been said on high authority that, if a husband or wife does not know of or suspect the other's adultery, that adultery cannot be said to have caused the desertion. But, with the greatest respect to the learned judges who have said this, is it correct? There are many things which a husband or wife who has been unfaithful may do or refrain from doing as a result of being unfaithful, and any one or more of those acts or omissions may cause the other spouse to leave. In such a case surely the petitioner would not have proved that the adultery had not caused the desertion, even though it was not known or suspected. Now, Mr Thursby, d'you think you're in a position to argue that point today?'

Whether I shall ever be, thought Roger, is most uncertain, but one thing is quite certain, I can't do it now. I must get help.

'I should be most grateful for an adjournment, my Lord,' he said.

'You shall have it,' said the judge. 'It isn't at all an easy point. Adjourned for fourteen days if that's convenient for you and many thanks for your help today.'

CHAPTER ELEVEN

Post Mortem

The judge went on with the next case and Roger, very hot and very red in the face, gathered up his papers and went out of the Court. There he was joined by Mrs Newent.

'What's all that in aid of?' she asked. 'Why haven't I got my divorce? What's happened?'

'It's a little difficult to explain,' said Roger.

'There's nothing difficult about it at all,' said Mrs Newent. 'It's what comes of having schoolboys to do one's case for one. I ought to have known from the start. How old are you, anyway?'

The humiliation was so great that Roger could have burst into tears. He felt like throwing his brief at Mrs Newent, running to the Embankment and jumping into the Thames. What was the good of anything? He wished the earth would swallow him up.

'Well, how old are you?' persisted Mrs Newent. Even at that stage of his misery Roger remembered for an instant the image he had built up of Mrs Newent before he met her, the poor girl abandoned by her callous husband. Now he was all on the side of Mr Newent. He wondered how he had stood her for as long as he had.

'Lost your voice?' said Mrs Newent. 'Not very much to lose anyway,' she added.

This at last spurred Roger into action.

'If you're not satisfied with the way I am doing your case, madam,' he said, with as much dignity as red-faced twenty-one could muster, 'you can ask your solicitors to instruct someone else to continue it. I do not propose to stand here listening to your abuse. Good morning.'

He left Mrs Newent with Mr Smith and went hurriedly to the robing-room. He still felt it was the end of the world. But, as he went, he went over in his mind the way the case had gone before Judge Ryman. What had he done wrong? Well, he had made mistakes once or twice, but they wouldn't have made any difference, surely? He had persuaded the judge that *Herod and Herod* applied – well, if he hadn't persuaded him, he'd at any rate mentioned *Herod* and the judge had gone into the matter. The judge had decided the first point of law in his favour. How on earth could he have imagined the second point would arise? Would anyone else have thought of it? Besides, the judge had thanked him for his help. He knew quite well he hadn't given any help, but the judge must think well of him to say it. But then the word 'schoolboys' started ringing in his ears again and he again had an urge to jump into the Thames.

'Warm, isn't it, sir?' said the attendant who helped him off with his gown.

'Yes,' said Roger. 'Very warm. Thank you.'

As he disrobed, he prayed that neither his mother, nor Sally nor Joy would be at the entrance to the Courts when he got out. He wanted to go and lock himself up somewhere out of sight of everyone. So this was the mighty Roger Thursby Esq, QC! Called a schoolboy by his own client! He looked through the window of the door of the robing-room to see if the coast was clear. It seemed to be. So he went out hurriedly and rushed across the Strand

in almost as fast a time as Mr Grimes usually put up. He
went back to chambers.

'Get on all right, sir?' asked Alec.

'I don't know. It's been adjourned.'

'When to?'

'Fourteen days, I think.'

'Why was that, sir? Witness missing?'

'No – I think he wants some point argued further.'

'I understand, sir,' said Alec, an expression into which
Roger read a wealth of meaning which was not in fact
there. As he started to go into his room, Henry came into
the clerks' room.

'Hullo,' he said. 'How did you get on?'

And then before Roger could reply, he went on: 'Like to
come and have a chat with me about it?'

Roger gratefully accepted and went into Henry's room,
where he told him as best he could what had happened in
Court.

'My dear chap,' said Henry, 'I think you did damned
well. Much better than I should have done at your age. I
shouldn't have been able to open my mouth. Jolly good
show. There's nothing to be depressed about. And you
seemed to have got on with old Ryman all right. He enjoys
an argument. All right, we'll give it him.'

'I shall never be able to argue,' said Roger miserably. 'I've
made a mess of it. I'm hopeless.'

'My dear old boy,' said Henry, 'if you could have seen me
coming away from my first County Court cases almost
sobbing, you wouldn't worry half so much. I used to lose
cases which quite definitely ought to have been won. All
the way home I used to try to convince myself that there
was nothing else that I could have done, but I knew
darned well there was. As far as I can see, you did
everything you could and you've got an adjournment to

get ready for the argument. That's very much better than I did in my first case.'

'I can't think you did worse,' said Roger.

'I did indeed,' said Henry. 'Mark you, it'll happen to you too. Or you'll be extraordinarily lucky if it doesn't. My only point is, it hasn't happened this time. Your case is still on its feet. You can win it yet. Or maybe in the Court of Appeal, if necessary.'

'Me in the Court of Appeal?' said Roger.

'Why not?' said Henry. 'They'll be very nice to you.'

'They'll need to be,' said Roger. 'But what was your first case?'

'Just a simple little accident case. Absolutely plain sailing. One just couldn't lose it. The defendant's driver had turned down a street which had stalls in the road and had then hit one of the stalls, damaged it and some of the stock. After the accident he said he was sorry but he'd misjudged the distance. Said that to a policeman. So there couldn't be any doubt about it. He was prosecuted for careless driving and fined. It was a sitter. The only question was the amount of damages and there I'd got evidence to prove everything up to the hilt. It was given to me because it was reckoned it was a case that couldn't be lost. The only reason the defendants were fighting it was because the insurance company doubted the amount of the damage. And, as I've told you, I could prove every penny of the damages and I did. The judge was quite satisfied about the damages. Oh, yes, it was the perfect case for a beginner. Excellent experience and no one could come to any harm. You couldn't lose it.'

Henry paused for a moment. 'I lost it all right,' he went on. 'I lost that perfect, unanswerable, copybook case. I lost it. The defendant's driver does a man twelve pounds worth of damage and what does the plaintiff get for it? The privilege of paying about twenty pounds costs in addition to bearing the whole of his own loss. And why? Because he briefed *me*. That's why. Simple enough.'

'But how did you come to lose it?'

'You may well ask. I'll tell you. No one actually saw the collision. The plaintiff heard a bang, looked round and saw his stall on the ground with the lorry half over it and half the stock ruined. Counsel for the defendant objected to the evidence of what the defendant's driver said to the policeman on the ground that the driver wasn't the agent of the defendant to make admissions. I didn't know what that meant but the judge said it was quite right and wouldn't allow that bit of evidence to be given. I wasn't so worried because, after all, the lorry had run into the stall, hadn't it? At the end of my case counsel for the defendant got up and calmly submitted that his client had no case to answer. No one had seen the accident, the driver might have had to swerve to avoid a child or a cyclist or anything. It was for the plaintiff to prove that the accident was due to the negligence of the defendant's driver. Well, although it was my first case, I thought I'd done rather well, because I'd brought down a case to quote to the judge if necessary. It was called *Ellor and Selfridge* and in it the Court held that where a motorist knocked somebody down on the pavement that was *prima facie* evidence of negligence as motor cars don't usually go on pavements. It was, therefore, for the motorist to show how he got there.

' "What do you say to that?" said the judge to my opponent.

' "The answer to that is quite simple," was the reply. "In *Ellor and Selfridge* the accident was on the pavement. I agree that lorries do not usually go on pavements, but here the accident was on the roadway. Lorries do go on roadways. It's the only place they do go. After the accident the lorry was still on the roadway. I don't complain about the plaintiff having a stall on the roadway, but he has it there at his risk. If an accident happens to it while it's in the roadway, he's got to prove that the accident was due to someone's fault. The mere fact that the accident happened doesn't prove that. As I said, it might have been due to some emergency."

' "Well, what do you say to that?" said the judge to me. I stammered and stuttered and got very red in the face. I said everything I could think of. I knew that if I could ever get the driver into the witness box I was bound to win because he would have to admit that there wasn't any emergency and that all that had happened was that he'd misjudged the distance. The thought that the defendant was going to get away with it was horrible. I did not become hysterical, but I felt like it. I said the same thing over and over again. The one thing I did *not* say was that if a lorry runs into a stationary stall on the highway, such an accident is normally caused by the fault of the lorry driver and it is therefore for him to explain how the accident happened, just as much as if the accident had happened on the pavement. The same would apply to an empty car which was standing stationary in broad daylight in the street. If it's run into it's obviously for the person who runs into it to explain how it happened. But I didn't say any of this, or think of it, till I was halfway back to the Temple. I just talked nonsense until suddenly the judge said: ' "Yes, I've got your point, Mr Blagrove. Do you want to add anything?"

'Well, of course, I sat down on that and the judge proceeded to give judgment against me.

' "Ask for leave to appeal," said the solicitor's clerk behind me.

'I did as I was told.

121

' "No," said the judge, "it's a plain case. I'm sorry for the plaintiff, but I can't let my judgment be blinded by sympathy. Leave to appeal refused."

'Well, you should have seen the plaintiff outside the Court after that. He was hopping mad at first. I don't blame him. And then he said something which I've never forgotten – he said it just as I was leaving him. He'd calmed down by then.

' "Hadn't you better do a bit more studying, boy, before you do your next case?" he said.

'He said it in quite a kindly tone. That made it worse. "I can't think," he went on, "the law's such an ass as all that." Well, of course, it isn't, but I was. And when I suddenly realized in the train on the way home what I ought to have said, I felt like jumping out on to the line, I can tell you. Then, of course, I started to explain to myself that it wouldn't have made any difference. One always ends up that way, but I knew it would really.'

'I must say, it's a relief to hear that,' said Roger, and he then told Henry what Mrs Newent had said.

'Of course, it is pretty dreadful for her to be represented by me,' he went on, 'when one comes to think of it. And I do look so young, too.'

'Well, you know my views on that,' said Henry. 'I don't think anyone should be allowed to address a Court until he's read for a year in chambers. But that isn't the case. And I'm quite sure you did as well as anyone with a first brief could have done. And you can still win, you know.'

'You've cheered me up no end,' said Roger. 'I suppose everyone feels like this to begin with.'

'Of course they do. We'll look up the point together if you like. I've nothing to do. Let's go and have lunch and then go to the Bar Library.'

Roger felt much better at the end of the day, but on the way home he wondered what his mother and Joy and Sally had thought of him. He found a note from Sally when he got home.

Well done, it said. Can I come and see you?

She ought to have been doing the case, thought Roger. She'd have told Mrs Newent a thing or two if she'd spoken to her like that. But then Mrs Newent wouldn't have spoken to her like that. There wouldn't have been any need to.

'You were simply perfect,' said his mother. 'I was so proud of you. You were quite the best-looking in the row.'

'How did you think I got on though?'

'Well, of course, darling, I don't know anything about law, but the judge seemed to do all the talking really. I suppose that's what he's there for.'

'I did say something, Mother, and, if you remember, the judge thanked me in the end.'

'Yes, I thought the judge awfully nice. I really would have liked to ask him to tea.'

'Mother,' said Roger in horror. 'You mustn't do anything of the sort. Promise you won't?'

'Of course, I won't, if you'd rather I didn't. But I would just like to drop him a note to thank him for being so sweet to you.'

Roger was very, very fond of his mother and he would never have cheerfully throttled her, but it was about the last straw. That's all she'd seen. The judge being sweet to him. And the worst of it was that it was no doubt true. The judge had been sweet to him and he looked like a schoolboy. All the good work done by Henry for a moment seemed to have been wasted. He was back where he started. But then he realized that his mother might write to the judge. So he had to say something.

'Mother', he said, 'you must promise not to do that either. The case is still going on. It would be most improper. You might get sent to prison and I might get disbarred.'

Just for the moment the idea of getting disbarred didn't seem too bad. He would go abroad and do whatever one does there.

'I was only joking, darling,' said his mother. 'You mustn't take everything so seriously. What a nice woman Mrs Newent seemed. I was so sorry for her.'

'Mrs Newent,' said Roger deliberately, 'is a bitch.'

'Roger!' said his mother. 'If that's the sort of language you are going to be taught at the Bar, I'm not sure that it's a good thing I let you start. Really, you quite took my breath away. It's not at all a nice word to use.'

'It's the only word,' said Roger, 'with which to describe Mrs Newent.'

'I can't think why you say that,' said his mother. 'Of course I didn't hear or understand half of what was said, but as far as I could make out, her husband had run off with one of the boarders. No, don't try and explain it, darling, I hate these legal technicalities and the sordid things that some husbands do. Not like your father, Roger. He was a very fine man. I thought you looked just like his pictures as a boy when I saw you in Court.'

'Thank you, darling,' said Roger. 'I'm so glad you were pleased. Now I must use the phone.'

He telephoned Joy.

'Roger, Roger darling. I was *so* thrilled. You were wonderful. I want to come right round now and kiss you, I'm so pleased. I never dreamed you'd be anything like that. You were quite perfect. And the judge thanking you at the end and everything. I'm so happy for you, I just don't know what to do. You'll have people coming to you to do their cases for them from everywhere. I'm sure Uncle Alfred will be terribly bucked. Oh, Roger – you are so clever. How do you do it?'

Knowing in his heart what the truth of the matter was, Roger did not take as readily to this eulogy as a young man might have been expected to do.

'Thank you very much, Joy. I don't think it was as good as all that, really.'

'Oh, but Roger, it was, it was. And, d'you know, the woman sitting next to me asked if I knew who you were. I said you were one of the most brilliant of the younger men.'

'Oh, you shouldn't have, Joy, really. What did she say?'

'Well, I didn't actually catch what she said. She had to speak awfully quietly, as you know, or we'd have been turned out. But I know she was impressed. Probably she's got a case coming on and she might even bring it to you. She was quite good-looking, Roger – but I shan't be jealous – not after last night.'

Oh, Lord! thought Roger. Last night. She hadn't forgotten. No, she wouldn't. But after all, I must be fair. She did get me the brief – this bloody, bloody brief, he suddenly said to himself. No, I must control myself. I wonder what Uncle Alfred thinks about it all.

At that moment Uncle Alfred, that is, Alfred Merivale, senior partner in Thornton, Merivale & Co, was having a word with his managing clerk, Mr Smith, who had been in Court with Roger.

'Don't make such a fuss, George,' he was saying. 'We'll just take in a leader next time.'

'Who's going to pay for it, sir?'

'Well, you aren't. So why should you worry?'

'Mrs Newent won't. She's livid, sir. Says it's our fault.'

'You are a miserable devil, George. I don't know how I've stood you for so long. Still we've got to have someone with a long face in the office. It's good for funerals and people drawing wills, I suppose. How d'you say the young man did?'

'He was quite hopeless, sir. I've seen some pretty good messes made of cases in the past, but that beat anything. My sympathies were all with the client, I can tell you. If I'd had someone appearing for me like that I think I'd have gone mad.'

'No one is appearing for you, George. And the case isn't over, anyway. Has he got a good presence, d'you think? You can't expect him to *say* anything yet.'

'Really, sir,' said George. 'I do think you ought to study the client a bit more. That case might have been lost today.'

'Well, it wasn't, George, it wasn't. I believe you'd have been pleased if it had been. No, I think I did make a slight mistake, but fortunately it's not too late to mend. We ought to have had someone to lead him in the first instance. After all, it was a discretion case and occasionally they go wrong. Yes, I ought to have thought of that. But it's so seldom, that I'm afraid I took a chance on it. And no harm's been done, George, no harm at all. On the contrary, I've learned a lesson. We must give him someone to lead him each time to begin with.'

'Why on earth d'you want to have him at all, sir?' grumbled George.

'If a very old great-uncle chooses to pander to his very sweet little great-niece – at his own expense, George – at his own expense, what the devil does it matter to you? It won't cost the client a penny more and the young man will get a nice lot of experience and quite a few guineas.' He paused for a moment and thought. 'Yes, George,' he went on, 'you're quite right to be down on me for taking a chance with this case, but all's well that ends well and only good has come of it. He's very young at the moment. D'you think we'll ever be able to send him into Court by himself?'

'He's quite well built,' said George. 'He could carry the books if the clerk's missing.'

Meantime, Joy was continuing to compliment Roger on his magnificent performance and she went on so long and so ecstatically that in the end Roger almost began to wonder if he had been so bad after all.

'I can't manage just now, Joy, dear – but could we meet for a drink or a walk or something about nine?'

'Where, darling?'

'The Pot-hole?'

'I'll be there, darling. Oh, Roger, I am so happy for you.'

A few minutes later he telephoned Sally.

'Thank you for your note, Sally. It was very sweet of you. Could I come and see you?'

'Of course. Mother's out at present. Excellent opportunity.'

He went round at once. She opened the door to him.

'Glad you're still in one piece,' she said.

'What d'you mean?' said Roger. He was still under the influence of Joy's remarks.

'Well, you did have a pretty rough time, didn't you? I thought you took it very well. I'd have wanted to run away.'

'You think I was rotten, I suppose,' said Roger, a trifle sulkily.

'Oh, Roger, don't be silly. I tell you, I don't know how you stood there at all. It was dreadful for you. Personally, I don't think it should be allowed.'

The spell was broken.

'That's what Henry says,' said Roger.

127

'Who's Henry?'

'Henry Blagrove. A chap in Grimes' chambers. I've told you about him, surely?'

'Oh, that one, the nice one. Yes, you have. Well, I'm glad someone else agrees with me. I shall get quite swollen-headed soon.'

'You mean about what the judge said?'

'I must say I was rather pleased, after our little talk. But really, Roger, I thought you took it splendidly. I thought you were going to break down once, but you didn't.'

'Really, Sally, there is a limit, you know.'

'Be honest, Roger. Didn't you feel like dropping your brief and running for it?'

Roger laughed.

'Why are you always so right, Sally? I've never known anyone like you – not any girl, anyway. Henry's rather like you as a matter of fact – except – except – '

He didn't finish the sentence.

'Except what, Roger?'

'Oh, nothing – forget it.'

'Except that he's kinder, Roger? Was that it?'

Roger said nothing. She was right again.

'But you see, Roger,' said Sally rather sadly, 'Henry doesn't happen to be in love with you.'

'Oh, Sally,' said Roger, 'I wish I knew if I loved you, I really do. Why don't you tell me if I do? You're always right. I'll believe you if you tell me.'

'I don't want to be right this time, Roger,' said Sally.

Neither of them spoke for a time after that. Roger broke the silence with: 'D'you think I'll ever improve, Sally?'

'D'you want to know what I really think?'

'Yes, of course,' he said quickly and then: 'No – I'm not sure if I do.' He thought for a moment. 'Better get it over,' he went on, 'let's have it. I can always sort football coupons.'

'Roger,' said Sally slowly, 'I think you're going to be a great man.'

'Sally, you don't, you don't really?' he said, fantastically excited, and then he suddenly choked. He'd have wept if he'd tried to say another word.

'But,' Sally went on quite calmly, 'there's a long way to go yet and you'll have to work terribly hard. You'll have a lot of disappointments, particularly because you're so young and don't understand anything yet. But you will, you will – and, barring accidents, you'll go to the top. I shall be quite pleased I once knew you.'

'Oh, Sally,' he said and burst into tears.

He went down on his knees and put his head in her lap. She stroked it gently.

'I love you, Sally, I love you. I know I do.'

'You don't, Roger, dear, though I love to hear you say it – and I'll always remember that you did – ' She stopped for a moment as though deliberately pigeon-holing the memory – then she went on. 'Roger dear, dearest Roger, you don't love anyone at the moment – except Roger.'

They remained for a little while in silence.

'Am I as bad as that?' he asked eventually. 'Just a selfish cad not minding who I hurt?'

'No, of course not,' she said more brightly. 'But you're young and ambitious and you like a good time too. And that's all there is to it. And why shouldn't you be like that? It's perfectly natural. Now, dry your eyes and give me a nice kiss. I won't read anything into it.'

CHAPTER TWELVE

Conference with Mr Merivale

The next day Mr Merivale himself made an appointment to see Roger.

'Good morning, young man,' he said after they had been introduced. 'I'm very grateful to you for all the work you've put into this rather troublesome little case of Newent.'

'Oh, thank you, Mr Merivale. I haven't done much good at present, I'm afraid.'

'Well,' said Mr Merivale, 'he's a difficult judge, she's a difficult client and it's not as simple a matter as I once thought. That's my fault, not yours. Quite frankly, young man, I think it was unfair of me to ask you to take the responsibility.'

'Oh, not at all. It was very good of you to send me the brief. I'm sorry I haven't done better with it. I imagine you'd like to give it to someone else now.'

'By no means,' said Mr Merivale, 'by no manner of means at all. I cannot think what could have put such an idea into your head.' He hesitated a moment and then said: 'You didn't see my clerk after the first hearing, I suppose?'

'No, I'm afraid I left in rather a hurry. Mrs Newent was rather offensive to me.'

'Well, that's all right then – I mean, I suppose she was a bit excited, but she shouldn't have been rude. But that's quite all right now. She quite understands the position and of course she wants you to go on with the case, of course she does. Be a fool if she didn't. I hear from my clerk that you put up a very stout performance – "for the ashes of your fathers and the temples of your gods." '

'I beg your pardon?' said Roger.

'Horatius, my boy. "And how can man die better than facing fearful odds – for the ashes of his fathers, etc, etc." Not that I'm suggesting you died, my boy. Far from it. Put up an excellent performance, excellent. Wish I'd been there to see it myself. I'll come next time, though, I really will.'

'I'm glad Mr Smith was pleased,' said Roger.

'Mr Smith was very pleased indeed,' said Mr Merivale. 'And I may tell you, young man, that Mr Smith is not a man who is easily pleased. Far, from it. Far from it. Particularly where counsel are concerned. No, I had a long talk with Mr Smith about you and I hope that in consequence we're going to see a lot more of you, my boy. We need young men like you these days. Fighters, that's what we want. Like your Mr Grimes, for instance. There are not many of them today. And there's a fighter for you. Never knows when he's beaten. D'you know, I've seen that man stand up in the Court of Appeal with the whole Court against him – all three of them – and battle with them for days. Another man would have sat down the first day.'

'And did he win, Mr Merivale?'

'No, my boy, I can't say that he won that particular case. But he went on three days and no one could have done more. Birkenhead himself couldn't have won it. Yes, that's the man for my money – my client's money, that is – a man who'll stand up to it, a man who's not frightened to tell the whole Court they're wrong – courteously, of course. But firmly and definitely and again and again, if necessary, until they almost have to throw him out by force. If a man's a fighter, I'll back him to the end. But they're very difficult to find today. Look at Marshall Hall, now, my boy. There was a fighter for you. Hardly knew a scrap of law, but it didn't matter. He'd thunder at the jury until they daren't convict his client. He'd never give up until the verdict had been returned. And, as often as not, it was in his client's favour. Of course, he couldn't win all his cases – no one could. Don't forget that, my boy, when you lose some. But fight, my boy, fight all the time. You don't mind an old man giving you a bit of advice, my boy?'

'I'm most grateful. I think it's very kind of you to take the trouble.'

'Now look,' went on Mr Merivale. 'This case of Newent. Between you and me, it's a tough 'un. It was bad of me not to realize it before. But we all make mistakes. That's how we learn. Now, I want you to do me a favour, my boy, a personal favour.'

'Why, certainly, Mr Merivale, of course I will.'

'It's just this. Newent's a case where in my considered opinion – my considered opinion, and of course I've been at it now for a good many years – Newent's a case where I think two heads will be better than one. I remember the late Lord Atkin saying that to me in his junior days – we used to brief him, you know – yes, and Mr Scrutton, as he then was – oh, yes, and others too. I flatter myself I've always known how to choose counsel – that's why I was so pleased to hear of you, my boy. I remember Atkin saying:

"Merivale," he said, "two of these," and he tapped his head, "are better than one."

' "Mr Atkin," I said, "there aren't two like yours in the world."

' "Well, then," he said, "get a leader with one as like it as you can find." He was a great man, a very great man, but d'you see, he decided in that particular case that two heads were better than one. You'd never have thought it possible that a man with his brain could want help from anyone, but, "this is a case for a leader, Mr Merivale," he said, and so a leader we had. And I'm going to make so bold in this case, young man, although I haven't the head of an Atkin – but just a few more years of experience than you perhaps, eh? I'm going to make so bold as to suggest that we have a leader in this case. Now, sir,' he added, 'now, sir, would you have any serious objections to our taking that course? If you have, say so, and it shan't be done. Mr Smith and I have absolute confidence in you, sir, absolute confidence. Those in fact were Mr Smith's very words. "Would you trust him again in Court, Mr Smith?" I asked. "I would," said Mr Smith, and he added – and mark this – "with something very heavy indeed." One doesn't often get remarks like that out of Mr Smith, I can tell you. And I don't mind adding, I was pleased, my boy, because I hadn't heard you myself. Now, what d'you say, my boy – you've only to say the word and we'll drop the idea altogether – but would you take a very old man's advice and – just as a favour to him – we get conceited, we old men, you know, and we like to think we're always right – would you, just to tickle my vanity – would you agree to our taking in a leader?'

'But, of course, Mr Merivale,' said Roger, who now had visions of a red bag, 'but, of course. I shall be only too pleased. As a matter of fact the judge said it was a difficult point – and now I come to think of it, Lord Atkin himself has said something about the matter.'

'Has he now?' said Mr Merivale. 'Has he indeed? Now that's most interesting. I shall study that with the greatest interest. Well, I'm delighted to hear you approve of the idea, my boy, delighted. And now all we've got to do is to choose our leader.'

He held up his hand.

'No, my boy, I know what you're going to say. It isn't etiquette for you to suggest a name? I wouldn't dream of infringing the rules, wouldn't dream of it. Just a few words with your clerk and hey presto, I shall think of the name that's escaped me for the moment. Now, my boy, I think that's all I've got to ask you at present, and I'm most grateful to you for seeing me at such short notice. It was most kind.'

'Not at all, Mr Merivale.'

'Well, goodbye, Mr – Mr Thursby – goodbye, and I shall look forward to attending a consultation with you and – and – now what was the name I was trying to think of?' and opening the door he went into the clerks' room. A few minutes later he came back again.

'Forgive my intruding again. I was just wondering' – he coughed and hesitated – 'I was just wondering,' he said again. 'I've got a young great-niece called Joyce – I believe you've met her – I was just wondering whether you'd care to dine with us next Friday – not a party, you know – quite informal – but Joy happens to be coming and with my daughter, who looks after me, it would make up the numbers. I hope you don't think it's a presumption on my part.'

'Of course not, Mr Merivale. It's most kind of you. I shall love to come. Oh, and I don't know if this is the right thing to say, but would you please thank Mr Smith for the kind remarks he made about me.'

'I shall not forget, my boy, I, shall not forget. Mr Smith shall be told.'

And Mr Merivale left.

CHAPTER THIRTEEN

Consultation

'Well, George,' said Mr Merivale when he was back in his office 'that's settled. The young man took it very well.'

'So should I take it very well,' said George, 'if someone told me I was going to be paid two or three times as much for doing nothing. Who are you going to have?'

'Plaistowe, I think,' said Mr Merivale, 'if he can take it.'

'And what's that going to cost you?'

'I don't know and I don't care. When you're an old man like me, you may find other ways of getting pleasure, though to look at you, George, one would think that you'll be looking for something as unpleasant as possible, but I know what I like and if I can pay for it, why shouldn't I have it?'

'I don't like to see money chucked away, sir. Plaistowe will want at least thirty. That means you'll have to pay that bright young specimen of yours twenty, sir. Really, sir, it goes against the grain to give him anything at all – but twenty really is the limit. Why, we could have got any of the best juniors at the Divorce Bar to do it for fifteen at the most, sir.'

'I sometimes wonder why you trouble to call me "sir," George. It normally is a sign of respect which I find in your case is lamentably lacking. I won't say that's always been so. Forty years ago you used to behave yourself quite well. You were a little frightened of me, I think. But now all you say to yourself is – "the old fool won't be here much longer, doesn't much matter what I do say. Anyway, I'm much too much use to the firm for them to fire me. I'm part of the furniture – which is solid, meant to last, and ugly." '

'I've the greatest respect for you, sir, but I hate to see you making a fool of yourself.'

'Well, I'm not. If I choose to spend fifty pounds or whatever it is on giving my niece a bracelet I can do so without asking you, can't I? Well, that's all I'm doing. Only she'll like this much more than a bracelet. Now don't let's have any more nonsense about it. Fix up a consultation with Plaistowe as soon as we know he can take it. I should say you'd better not have the client there in the first instance. He can see her later if he wants to. You'd better attend it as you saw what happened in Court.'

'I did indeed, sir,' said George. 'I shall have great pleasure in telling Mr Plaistowe all about it.'

'Now, George, you're to behave yourself. It's not young Thursby's fault. It's mine, if you like. Well, you've taken it out of me, don't try to take it out of him too. Come to think of it, I'll come with you to see fair play. I'm not going to have him bully-ragged. Joy would be very cross indeed and she'd be fully justified.'

'P'raps you'd like to go by yourself, sir,' said George.

'Now, George, don't sulk. Of course you must be there to put Plaistowe in the picture. I'm only coming to see that you don't make it too lurid.'

'As you please, sir,' said George. 'I'm only an unadmitted managing clerk and I know my place.'

'Whose fault is it you're not a partner? You could have had your articles years ago.'

'I knew my place then and I know it now. I don't believe in all this partner business. My job's a managing clerk, I know it and I can do it, and that's how it's going to stay.'

'By all means, George, but as that's how you want it, don't grizzle.'

A few days later a consultation was arranged with Plaistowe, a busy common law silk who did a certain amount of divorce work and was known to be exceptionally able. His fees were extremely moderate for a man of his ability and in consequence he was very much in demand. Before the consultation began Plaistowe asked to see Roger. They shook hands.

'How are you, my dear chap? I don't think we've met before. You're in Grimes' chambers, I believe?'

'I'm his pupil, as a matter of fact,' said Roger. 'I've only been there just over a week.'

'Got away to a flying start, eh? Good for you. I thought I'd just have a word with you about this before we saw the clients. I gather the lady's not here today. But she's given all her evidence – unless we want something more out of her – so that's all to the good. I gather we don't care for her very much.'

'No,' said Roger.

They talked about the case for a short time and then Mr Merivale and Mr Smith were shown in.

'How are you, Mr Merivale? It's a long time since we met. Not since I took silk, I believe.'

'Ah, I don't very often come to the Temple nowadays, Mr Plaistowe, but in this case Mr Smith – whom, of course, you know, particularly wanted me to come. So, as I have to do what I'm told, here I am and very pleased to see you again.'

Plaistowe shook hands with Mr Smith and they all sat down.

138

'I gather our client's a bit of a so-and-so,' said Plaistowe. 'D'you think the judge believed her?' Plaistowe looked first at Roger and then at Mr Smith. Roger cleared his throat.

'I think probably Mr Smith will know that better than me – with all his experience.'

Mr Merivale looked at Mr Smith with something of an air of triumph, which seemed to say, 'Not quite such a fool as you thought, eh, George?'

'He won't believe her where he can help it, sir,' said Mr Smith. 'But I don't think he's going to down us on that. He doesn't like the nearness of the adultery to the desertion, and he's not satisfied that the mere fact that the husband didn't know is enough. Would you agree with me, sir?' and he turned to Roger.

'It sounded rather like it,' said Roger.

'Well, do we want any more evidence from our client? What d'you say, Mr Merivale?' asked Plaistowe.

'I think you'd better put that to Mr Smith. I'm really only here as I've said because he asked me to come. I don't really know much about it, except that your learned junior has so far done admirably, as Mr Smith will confirm.'

Plaistowe caught Mr Smith's eye and quickly said: 'I'm quite sure he will. Well, what d'you say, Mr Smith? Is there any point in trying to get any more out of our client?'

'Quite candidly,' said Mr Smith, 'the less we see of that lady in the witness box – or indeed anywhere else – the better. He caught her out in a thumping lie and although he hasn't said anything about it at the moment, knowing Judge Ryman, I'm pretty sure it's in safe keeping.'

'Then you think just argue the point of law that there must be desertion if there's no knowledge of the adultery?'

'Yes, sir,' said Mr Smith, 'that's my opinion, but, of course, Mr Thursby here may have different views. From what I gathered during his address to the judge, as far as I was able – '

'Yes, Mr Thursby,' interrupted Mr Merivale, 'and what is your opinion? My recollection is that, when I saw you in chambers, you were of precisely the same opinion as Mr Smith has just expressed, though Mr Smith won't mind my saying that I thought you put it rather better.'

'I wouldn't say that at all,' said Roger, 'but for what it is worth, that is my opinion.'

'I'm glad you confirm Mr Smith's view,' said Mr Merivale. 'It's always satisfactory to the lowly solicitor when counsel agrees with him. Alas, it is not so often, I fear.'

'You're too modest,' said Plaistowe. 'I nearly always agree with solicitors – when they're right.'

CHAPTER FOURTEEN

Sally

Sally's mother lay on a couch with her eyes closed. Sally came into the room but her mother took no apparent notice. Sally sat down and opened a paper and rustled it. Her mother's eyes remained closed. After waiting a few minutes, Sally said quite softly: 'Mother, darling, are you with Brahms?'

There was no answer and the eyes remained closed. So Sally went on reading. After a few minutes Mrs Mannering opened her eyes.

'No, Schubert, darling,' she said. 'What is it you want?'

'Could you bear to be separated for a moment?' asked Sally.

'He turned me out,' said her mother. 'Said he had an appointment with someone or other. I forget the name. No. I remember. Georges Sand.'

'That was Chopin, Mother.'

'My darling Sally, you must allow me to dream whom I choose. It was Georges Sand. As a matter of fact he said she was leaving Chopin.'

'Dates, Mother.'

'There are no dates in dreams, darling, not in mine anyway. But you look serious. What is it?'

'D'you think I'd be silly to change my job, Mother?'

'You're in love with that young man, aren't you?' replied her mother.

'Terribly.'

'How will changing your job help?'

'I thought – I thought,' began Sally and for once spoke with less confidence and started to blush as she said it: 'I thought of going into a solicitor's office.'

'I see,' said her mother, and thought for a moment. 'That certainly makes sense.' She paused again. 'But is it any good, Sally? Have you any chance?'

'Oh, Mother, darling, I just don't know. Not at the moment, certainly, not a hope at the moment. But you can't be absolutely sure. And I'd wait for years and years if need be.'

'You'd be very good for him,' said her mother. 'You'd make a nice pair. But he's terribly young, of course. Still, he'll grow. Of course, you're not all that old, though I agree that every one of your twenty-one years is equal to two of his. But that's usually so with girls.'

'I'm sure he's not really fond of Joy,' said Sally. 'She's much prettier than I am, of course, but she's such a little ass, he couldn't be.'

'I don't believe that's a criterion,' said her mother. 'There are lots of sweet little asses in the world, male and female, and highly intelligent people fall in love with them, marry them and live happily with them ever after.'

'I suppose that's right,' said Sally, 'but I'm not really worried about Joy. Except for one thing.'

'What's that?'

'She might buy him.'

'What a horrible thing to say. You can't love a man who'll hand himself over to the highest bidder.'

'He wouldn't know he was doing it. As you say, he's terribly young. He's very impressionable and – and very ambitious. If Joy can get her uncle to feed him with briefs – '

'Sally, this is really becoming unpleasant. You are actually proposing to start an auction. I realized it was something to do with Roger, of course, but I didn't realize you were seriously thinking of going into the market yourself.'

'Well – that's why I wanted to talk to you. Do you really think it's dreadful? If Joy didn't brief him, I wouldn't. But if she does, why shouldn't I? Why should she have such a huge advantage? Why, out of mere gratitude he might feel he had to marry her. That really is dreadful, if you like.'

'And suppose you send him bigger and better briefs than Joy – suppose you outbid her at every turn, two for each of her one, ten guineas where she sends five, the Court of Appeal when she sends him to the County Court, the House of Lords when she sends him to the Court of Appeal – '

'Don't, Mother,' said Sally, 'there's no need to make it sound beastlier than it is. All right, it is beastly if you like. But I wouldn't let him marry me out of gratitude. I should know and I wouldn't. He did sort of ask me to marry him once, but I wouldn't say "Yes" then as I know he wasn't sure. I'll only marry him if he really wants me – but oh, Mother darling, I do want him to.'

'You certainly have got it badly, Sally.'

'You let Father accompany you, Mother, and it was torture. Wasn't that bidding for him?'

'You have a point there, Sally. That odious creature Nellie – what was her name? Thank Heaven – I've forgotten it. She used to let him play and she had a voice like an angel. What could I do? I wasn't in her class. But my wrong wouldn't make your wrong right.'

'But you weren't wrong Mother, darling. You were right. Look how happy you were – it can't have been wrong. He'd have been most unhappy with Nellie what's-her-name. You'll admit that, won't you? And you had all those years of happiness together and you produced a most efficient, intelligent, not too bad-looking – and entirely miserable little girl. I'm going to do it, Mother darling. You did and I'm going to. It's sweet of you to make things so clear to me. Now you can go back to Brahms, sorry, Schubert.'

She lifted her mother's legs on to the sofa again.

'Back you go,' she said. 'P'raps he's tired of Georges Sand by now.'

The same afternoon Sally obtained a secretarial job with Messrs Moodie and Sharpe to start in a fortnight's time when she had completed her period of notice with her employers.

'Have you any experience of legal work, Miss Mannering?' asked Mr Sharpe, the partner who saw her, after she'd given satisfactory proof of her shorthand and typing ability.

'Not really,' said Sally, 'but I've been to the Courts once and I've got a friend who's a barrister.'

'Oh, who's that?'

'Oh, you wouldn't know him. He's only a pupil. Just started. He's with a Mr Grimes.'

'Oh, I know *him* well. We brief him sometimes, as a matter of fact. That's very interesting. And why do you want to come to a solicitor's office?'

'I like the law and, who knows, I might become a solicitor myself in the end, if I were good enough.'

'And then you could send briefs to your friend – Mr – Mr – I don't think you mentioned the name?'

Sally blushed slightly.

'It's Thursby, as a matter of fact,' she said. 'Roger Thursby.'

'You needn't feel embarrassed, Miss Mannering. It's quite a normal thing. I advised a client of mine to send his daughter to be articled to a solicitor. She was going to marry a barrister. A jolly good partnership, I thought, unless they went in for more productive schemes. Even then they can sometimes be combined. Oh – no – you mustn't flatter yourself that you're the first to think of that.'

'Thank you for being so frank, Mr – er – Mr Sharpe.'

'Thank you, Miss Mannering, and would you like to start today fortnight? Good. You'll be working for me. My secretary's leaving to get married. No, not a barrister. Oh, by the way, I ought to warn you that I'm on the conveyancing side. I don't do any litigation.'

'I see,' said Sally. 'All the same, I'd like to come, please.'

'Excellent. I think we should suit each other very well. And don't worry too much about the conveyancing. I have a most understanding partner. But he won't send briefs to people who aren't any good. Has an old-fashioned notion about studying the interests of the client. Oh, there is just one other thing. I hope you won't mind or feel offended. It's purely a formality. I'd just like you to meet my wife first.'

'I see,' said Sally.

'It's much better that way,' said Mr Sharpe. 'She'll pass you without a doubt.'

'Indeed,' said Sally.

'She has an almost pathological aversion to blondes. That's all I meant, I assure you.'

CHAPTER FIFTEEN

Newent v Newent

In due course Mrs Newent's petition came on again for hearing. This time Roger was in a state of the happiest excitement. He was going to sit behind a QC. And he had only been called a little over a month. He wouldn't have to open his mouth in Court, but he'd be one of the counsel in the case, he was getting an enormous fee of twenty guineas, nearly three times as much as was marked on his original brief. He even wondered for a moment if he'd get both the seven and the twenty guineas, but he dismissed the thought as unworthy. Since the consultation he had spent many hours looking up authorities and he eventually had delivered a voluminous note to Plaistowe.

'Not at all bad, my dear chap. Difficult to believe you've only just been called.'

'I had a bit of help from a man in my chambers called Blagrove.'

'I see. Henry doing some work for a change. Never mind. Tell him I've marked it Beta plus. That'll shake him.'

Mrs Newent came to the Court to watch. Her anger had been assuaged by Mr Merivale and she was quite pleased at the idea of being represented by a QC. That would be something to talk about afterwards, particularly to her friend who'd only had a junior.

At 10.20 Roger was duly installed in Court waiting for his leader to arrive. Suddenly his inside dropped to the ground, just as it had done when the case had been transferred from Judge Crane to Judge Ryman. He had seen Alec and Plaistowe's clerk deep in conversation together. Then to his horror they approached Mr Merivale and asked him to come outside. Roger had by this time seen enough of the Bar to know that even a QC cannot be in two places at once. And if, for example, a case in a higher Court in which Plaistowe happened to be involved had unexpectedly not finished he might have to stay on and finish it. Suddenly Roger remembered having seen Plaistowe's name in *The Times* a few days before in a case in the House of Lords. He broke into a sweat. He was going to have to do it again. He hadn't even thought of the possibility. He had at any rate seen the cases, but it was hopeless for him to try and argue with a judge like Ryman. This time neither Sally nor Joy nor his mother were present, but their absence gave him no consolation. The Court was crowded and it would be awful; even if it had been empty it would have been just as bad. He had been so happy at the thought of sitting back and hearing how the case should be conducted and now he was going to have to do it himself – and, of course, he'd lose it. At that moment in his misery Alec came into Court, reached in front of him, said: 'Excuse me, sir,' and took away his brief. Fear was now replaced by utter gloom. They were going to take the brief away from him. Not that he could blame them, but that's what was going to happen. They'd already done it. How terribly humiliating! As if he hadn't had enough already. The fates were being very unkind. What would he say to Sally and Joy? He'd look such a fool. Oh, well – there was always sorting football coupons. He was interrupted in these miserable thoughts by Alec, who replaced the brief in front of him. On it he saw that what had once been marked as twenty guineas was now thirty-three. All the conference between the clerks had been about was an increase in the fee. Plaistowe's clerk thought that fifty guineas would be more appropriate to the occasion than thirty. So Roger had to have thirty-three whether he liked it or not. He sang to himself: 'What was once down-drip is now up-drip.' He could have wept for joy – and nearly did. A few minutes later Plaistowe arrived and Roger's happiness was complete.

Then the judge sat and the case was called on. Plaistowe got up.

'May it please your Lordship, this petition in which I now appear with my learned friend, Mr Thursby – ' Those words sounded very good to Roger. What a pity Sally couldn't have heard them. And Joy too, of course. After all, it was entirely through her that it had happened at all. And he'd have liked his mother there, too, though she wouldn't have appreciated the importance of the occasion. But he mustn't think of things like that. He must see how Plaistowe dealt with the case.

'Yes, I remember, Mr Plaistowe. It was adjourned for further argument. I'm very glad to have your help in the matter, though this remark is not intended as any disparagement of your learned junior.'

'Thank you, my Lord.'

Plaistowe then went on to recall the facts to the judge's mind and then to argue on the point of law. He quoted every case which had any possible bearing on the matter. He laid particular emphasis on the passages which supported his contentions, and eventually when he could do no more, he sat down.

Judge Ryman arranged the papers in front of him and proceeded to give judgment. Among other things he said this: 'I am bound in this Court to hold contrary to my own belief that it is at present the law of England that a man or woman who commits adultery remains entitled to the comfort and society of the other spouse so long as the adultery is sufficiently well concealed. But although I am bound to hold in this Court that adultery does not automatically prevent desertion, the petitioner must prove that the deserting party would have deserted anyway and that the adultery had nothing whatever to do with it. In my opinion, where the parties are living together, the acts or omissions or words of an adulterous spouse may, without amounting to neglect or misconduct, set in motion a train of events which breaks up the marriage. The wife returning from her lover may, as a result of a guilty conscience, say something to her husband or may even look at him in a way which starts an altercation. That altercation may lead to further disagreements and eventually the innocent spouse may leave the other. How can it then be said that just because the deserting spouse did not know of or suspect the adultery, the adultery had nothing to do with the desertion? In a case where the adultery was many years previously and there had been a long history of a happy marriage with children being born thereafter, no doubt it could be said that, when twenty years later the wife left her husband, her desertion had nothing to do with the very remote act of adultery. But conversely when the act of adultery is close to the desertion, I should have thought that it would be very difficult indeed for a petitioner to satisfy a Court that the adultery did not cause the desertion. In the present case the adultery *was* very close to the desertion. It may be that it caused it. I do not say it did. I do not know. And that means that the petitioner has certainly not proved to my satisfaction that her adultery had nothing to do with it. In the result, I hold that desertion has not been proved and the petition must be dismissed.'

Well, thank Heaven, thought Roger, it wasn't my fault this time.

'Well, Mrs Newent,' said Plaistowe outside the Court. 'We shall have to consider whether to advise you to appeal. My personal opinion is that the judge is right, but, on the whole, I think that the Court of Appeal will take a different view.'

'That's all Greek to me,' said Mrs Newent. 'And I didn't understand what the judge was saying either. But I've lost my case, have I?'

'You have at the moment.'

'And I'm still married to that so-and-so?'

'Yes.'

'Well, all I can say is, I wish him joy of it. I've had enough of the law. *He* can try next time. I don't know what all the fuss is about. My friend got her divorce all right. So why shouldn't I? It isn't justice.'

'I'm extremely sorry, Mrs Newent,' began Plaistowe.

'Not half as sorry as I am,' said Mrs Newent. 'Cost me a pretty penny and what have I got for it? Nothing.'

She looked round for a moment as though trying to see whom she could blame. Her eye came to Roger.

'If you ask me,' she went on, 'it's all come about by employing schoolboys to do my case. If I'd had a proper barrister in the first instance this would never have happened.'

'You've no right to talk like that,' said Plaistowe.

'No right, haven't I? It's a free country and I can say what I like. Of course you all stand together. You would. But if you want my opinion you're all a bloody lot of twisters and that's straight.'

150

'Come along, my dear chap,' said Plaistowe to Roger. 'Goodbye, Mr Merivale, Mr Smith. Let me know if I can be of any further help to you.'

And so ended Roger's first case with a leader. He was secretly glad that Mrs Newent had started to abuse Plaistowe in much the same way as she had abused him, and that Plaistowe's reaction had been similar to his own. He wondered if Plaistowe would send him a red bag. He did not expect one, but it was nice to think of the possibility.

CHAPTER SIXTEEN

Wrap It Up

It remained a possibility for a time, but not for very long. Plaistowe did in fact consider it but decided that it would be a bad precedent and possibly not very good for Roger, though he thought him a pleasant and potentially able young man. After the tumult and the shouting about *Newent and Newent* had died down and Roger had told everyone about it, he returned to the normal life of a pupil with Mr Grimes. He looked at untold numbers of briefs. He went regularly into Court, he made notes in Court which sometimes Mr Grimes actually looked at. He turned up points of law in the Bar Library, he started to prepare those technical legal documents called pleadings as an exercise and then looked to see how Mr Grimes did them himself; he went and had coffee at Grooms, he lunched in the Crypt, in counsel's room in the Law Courts and very occasionally in hall. He often went to the 'Bear Garden' and he followed Mr Grimes about as fast as he could and he asked Henry innumerable questions. Sometimes he had that terrible sinking feeling in the stomach when he was in Court with Mr Grimes and saw Alec hovering about waiting to pounce on his master to drag him to some other Court, leaving perhaps Roger to hold the fort while he was away. But this did not actually happen for some months after his first day, though the fear of it was often there. Among other things he frequently went to the hearing of applications to adjourn cases. Mr Grimes often had to make such an application and one day, when it seemed as though he might be held up in the Privy Council and that no one else would be available, Roger was asked by Alec to be prepared to apply to the judge in charge of the non-jury list for a case to be stood out of the list. The application was consented to by the other side, but that did not necessarily mean that it would be granted. If cases about to come on for trial could be taken out of the list at will the lists would get into hopeless disorder. Some judges are fairly easy about granting applications which are consented to. Some are not so easy. Some are very difficult, particularly when the reason for the adjournment is simply that the parties are not ready. As usual Roger consulted Henry on the subject.

'Who is the judge?'

'Bingham, I think.'

'That's bad. He's the worst. You must wrap it up.'

'What's that mean?'

'Have you never heard of old Swift?'

'Only by name really. What about him?'

'I'll tell you. He was a judge with an attractive accent all of his own, though with a north country bias and a rather slow way of speaking. He would pronounce "Mister" rather like "Mistah" and "o" in "of" rather like "u" in "up." He was a very popular judge, though he was very much master in his own Court. No one could take liberties with Swift. He could be very awkward if he wanted to and he was naughty sometimes. He could also be very helpful if he wanted to be, particularly to a young man. He had an amusing sense of humour. The story goes that one day Swift was hearing applications for adjournments when a

153

young man called Croft with a very white wig got up and asked leave to mention the case of *Smith* against *Brown*.

' "What is your application, Mistah Cruft?" said Swift.

' "It's by consent, my Lord, to take the case out of the list for fourteen days, my Lord."

' "On what grounds, Mistah Cruft?" said Swift.

' "Oh, my Lord, I don't think the parties are quite – "
'Before he could say any more Swift intervened.

' "Wrap it up, Mistah Cruft," he said.

' "I beg your pardon, my Lord?" said young Croft, completely mystified.

' "Wrap it up," repeated Swift.

'Croft just looked miserable – I believe you know the feeling – and thereupon Swift said rather sternly, but with a twinkle in his eye: "Sit down, Mistah Cruft, and listen to Mistah Andrew Pain. You have an application, I believe, Mistah Andrew Pain?"

' "Yes, my Lord – in the case of *Hatchett and Bellows* which is No. 1357 in the non-jury list."

' "What is your application?"

' "To stand the case out for a month, my Lord."

' "And the grounds?"

' "Oh, my Lord, the action is for breach of an oral contract. One of the witnesses to the making of the contract is in Brazil and can't be back for at least three weeks. At the time the case was set down it was not known by anyone that he would have to go there, but unfortunately only recently the witness' aged mother who is staying in Brazil became ill and he had to go to her. Then, my Lord, another reason for the adjournment is that through no fault of the parties or their solicitors some of the documents in the case were burnt. They are vital documents and the solicitors are trying to reach agreement as to what they contained. Then, my Lord, another witness, or I should say a possible witness, has suddenly left his address and we haven't been able to trace him yet. Finally, my Lord, one of the partners in the firm of solicitors instructing me has unfortunately just gone into hospital for appendicitis and the managing clerk who was attending to the matter has gone to another firm."

' "Mistah Cruft," said Swift.

'Pain was still on his feet, and his application not yet disposed of, so Croft, who was, of course, sitting down, thought he might have misheard and remained seated.

' "Mistah Cruft," said Swift loudly and sternly.

Croft rose trembling to his feet.

' "Mistah Cruft, did you hear Mr Andrew Pain's application?"

' "Yes, my Lord."

' "That's what I call wrapping it up," said Swift.'

CHAPTER SEVENTEEN

Criminal Proceedings

Occasionally, though not very often, Mr Grimes appeared in a Criminal Court and Roger, of course, went with him. Peter always went on these occasions because, as he said, that was more in his line. On one such occasion Mr Grimes had a big conspiracy case in which he was prosecuting on behalf of a large company. Such cases always start in the Magistrate's Court and the day before the first hearing Roger mentioned it to Henry.

'I wonder if you'll be before old Meadowes,' said Henry. 'I hope so. He's an amusing old bird sometimes.'

'Come on,' said Roger. 'Let's have it – I can go to the Bar Library when you've told me.'

'Well, Meadowes had an old hand up in front of him who rather liked going to prison in the winter. He had a pretty hard life and he found prison more comfortable in the cold weather. So, regularly every October he'd commit some crime worth six months, do his stretch and come out in the spring. Well, one day this old boy came up in front of Meadowes. He pleaded guilty as usual, said he had nothing to say and waited for the usual six months.

' "Three months imprisonment," said Meadows.

'The old boy thought he must have misheard.

' "What's that?" he said.

' "Three months imprisonment," repeated the clerk.

' "But that's all wrong, your Worship. I always get six months for this."

' "Take him away," said the clerk.

'The old boy clung to the bars of the dock.

' "But please, your Worship, make it six. I always get six for this, straight I do."

'A policeman started to remove him from the dock.

' "Leave me alone, you something something," said the old man. "I have my rights."

' "Now, look," said Meadowes, who thought he had better take a hand, "if you don't behave yourself, I shan't send you to prison at all!" '

At that moment Alec came into the room.

'Mr Grimes would like to see you, sir,' he said to Roger.

'How are ye, my dear fellow,' said Mr Grimes when Roger arrived. 'Now look, my dear fellow, will ye very kindly keep this case in the Magistrate's Court back till I arrive tomorrow. It'll be quite all right, my dear fellow. I've spoken to Brunner who's on the other side and he's agreeable. All ye have to do is to tell the clerk before the magistrate sits, and then wait till I come. If by accident it's called on before I come, just ask the magistrate to keep it back.'

'You will be there, I suppose?' said Roger, who had learned a good deal now by experience.

'Of course I'll be there, my dear fellow, of course I'll be there. What are ye thinking of? Of course I'll be there. Dear, dear, dear – not be there, who ever heard of such a thing, dear, dear, dear.'

'Suppose it is called on and the magistrate won't keep it back?'

'Just tell him the tale, my dear fellow, just tell him the tale.'

'But what tale?'

'Look, my dear fellow,' said Mr Grimes, 'if ye don't want to do it, ye needn't. I can get Hallfield to do it. But I thought ye might like it, my dear fellow, I thought ye might like it.'

'Oh, I should very much.'

'That's right, my dear fellow, that's the way, that's the way. Ye have seen the papers, have ye?'

'I've looked at them, but not very thoroughly.'

'Well, ye'd better look at them again now, my dear fellow. Ye'll find lots of tales to tell from them, my dear fellow. Oh, dear, yes. It's a fine kettle of fish. Taking machinery from under their very noses. I don't know what we're coming to, my dear fellow, I really don't. They'll be stealing houses next and factories. They took half the contents of one in this case. And from under their very noses, under their very noses. I don't know, my dear fellow, but there it is. They will do these things, they will do these things.'

Roger took the papers away. The case was about a large conspiracy to steal. Roger wondered if he'd ever be able to master a brief of that size, though he had more confidence in being able to do so than he had three months previously.

The next day he went to the Magistrate's Court in plenty of time and saw the clerk before the magistrate sat.

'That's a bit awkward,' said the clerk. 'The lists are in a complete mess today. He's taking some summonses after the charges but there aren't many of them and they won't last long. Can't you start it?'

'I'd rather not,' said Roger.

'I thought that's how you got experience at the Bar,' said the clerk. 'When I was practising as a solicitor they used to play it on me like blazes. Sometimes I'd get the most awful damn fools appearing for part of the case when I'd briefed someone quite good. But it's jolly good experience for the young chaps who come down. Not such a pleasant experience for the solicitor sometimes, or easy to explain to the client.'

'Yes, it must be difficult, I agree. D'you think you'll be able to keep this case back, though?' asked Roger anxiously. 'I'm sure the solicitor will be furious if I do it. I'm only a pupil, you know.'

'Splendid,' said the clerk. 'I suppose it's the nasty part of my nature coming out. I love to see it happening to other people. Watch the client squirm while you make a mess of it – not that you'd make a mess of it, I'm sure, Mr – Mr – '

'Thursby's my name,' said Roger, 'and I can be guaranteed to make a complete mess of it. So if that's what you want, call the case and you'll have a whale of a time.'

Roger was surprised at his own self-confidence. The clerk laughed.

'Well, that's the first time I've heard counsel talk like that. Good for you, if I may say so, and if you don't mind an older man, albeit a solicitor, saying this – if you stick to that attitude of mind you'll have a darned good chance of getting on. It's these smart alecs and know-alls who come croppers. Good for you. Very glad to have met you. I'll keep the old boy back even if he starts dancing round the room.'

'That's awfully good of you,' said Roger. 'I'm most grateful. Sorry to have done you out of a good laugh though. One day p'raps I'll have a brief of my own and then you'll be able to make up for it.'

It was the first time Roger had been to a magistrate's court and he watched the proceedings with interest. First came the overnight charges, the drunks, the prostitutes, the suspected persons, and so forth.

'Were you drunk and incapable?'
'Yes.'
'Facts, officer.'
Facts stated.
'Anything known?'
'Not for this, your Worship.'
'Anything to say?'
Nothing.
'Ten shillings, please.'

And so on to the next case. The speed at which the magistrate got through his work astounded Roger and, after a morning at his Court, he thought that, if as he supposed, every Court had much the same amount to do, it was a great tribute to the care and ability of London magistrates that so few people complain of their cases not being properly heard. But he wondered what would happen if there were a concerted scheme on the part of the public to plead Not Guilty. It would cause chaos. As it was, most of those charged or summoned pleaded Guilty. It seems a pity all the same, he thought, that criminal cases have to be tried at such a rate. He had started to work out in his mind what the cost to the country of a few extra magistrates and courts would be, when his attention was distracted from this calculation by the case of Cora. She was a demure-looking person and when she went into the dock she looked modestly down at her feet. The charge was read out and she was asked if she pleaded Guilty or Not Guilty. She started to say 'Guilty' when she looked up and saw who the magistrate was. Metropolitan Courts have at least two magistrates, sometimes sitting alternate days, sometimes in separate Courts on the same day. She had arrived late and thought that someone else would be sitting.

'Oh, no,' she said, 'Not Guilty. Not Guilty at all. I should say not,' and she added under her breath something which the jailer could hear but the magistrate, who was old and slightly deaf, could not. What she said was: 'Not with you there, you old stinker.'

'What was that?' asked the magistrate.

'I didn't quite catch, your Worship,' said the jailer, after a slight cough.

'Didn't know it was me, was that it?' asked the magistrate.

'Something like that, your Worship,' coughed the jailer.

'Oh, I only wanted the sense, thank you,' said the magistrate. 'Very well. Take the oath, officer.'

Roger discovered the reason for the sudden change in Cora's attitude. Most magistrates fine prostitutes forty shillings and that's the end of the matter. They pay this about once a fortnight and the amount is only a trifle out of their considerable earnings. That is the maximum penalty that can be imposed. But there is power under an old Act – some six hundred years old – to call upon them to find sureties for their good behaviour with the alternative of a term of imprisonment. No prostitute can find such sureties, whether she is on her own or run by a man. If she is on her own, she would not normally know any who would stand as surety; if she is controlled by a man, the man who controls her would not mind losing his twenty-five pounds or whatever it was when the condition of the recognizance was broken, as, of course, it would be – but he does not want to advertise his relationship to the girl. In consequence in almost every instance of a prostitute being called upon to find sureties for her good behaviour, she goes to prison instead. Mr Meadowes was wont to adopt this course and, as often as not, prostitutes who were to appear before him simply did not turn up, but came on another day when there was another magistrate. Cora had made a mistake. As soon as she saw it she changed her plea to 'Not Guilty' just in time. Roger wondered whether the police would be able to establish, as they had to, that people who had been solicited by Cora had been annoyed. It could not be altogether an easy task, he thought, as none of the men solicited would be likely to give evidence. In Cora's case the material evidence was as follows:

POLICE OFFICER: 'At the corner of Regent Street I saw the accused approach a man. She smiled at him and said something. He walked away hurriedly. Five minutes later at about the same spot she approached another man. He spoke to her for a minute and then went away. He appeared annoyed. A few minutes later she approached another man. He apparently saw her coming and avoided her. I then arrested the accused. She said, "Take your hands off me, you filthy stinker. Why don't you go after some of the French girls. They drop you too much, I suppose." At the police station she was charged and said: "You're all a lot of stinking so-and-so's." '

THE CLERK (To CORA): 'Do you want to ask the officer any questions?'

CORA: 'I'll say. That first man you say I spoke to, how d'you know I didn't know him?'

POLICE OFFICER: 'He didn't appear to know you. He walked off hurriedly.'

CORA: 'He may not have liked me.'

MAGISTRATE: 'Next question.'

CORA: 'You say the next man was annoyed, how do you know?'

POLICE OFFICER: 'He seemed annoyed.'

MAGISTRATE: 'How did he show his annoyance?'

POLICE OFFICER: 'He just seemed annoyed, your Worship.'

CORA: 'What at?'

POLICE OFFICER: 'Because you solicited him.'

CORA: 'How do you know that?'

POLICE OFFICER: 'There couldn't have been any other reason.'

CORA: 'I might have asked him for a light.'

POLICE OFFICER: 'He didn't put his hand in his pocket.'

CORA: 'Well, of course, he wouldn't if he didn't have a match, would he? You didn't hear what I said, did you?'

POLICE OFFICER: 'No, but you smiled at him.'

CORA: 'Is that a crime? Don't you smile at anyone?'

MAGISTRATE: 'You needn't answer that question.'

CORA: 'Well, I want him to.'

MAGISTRATE: 'I don't. Next question.'

CORA: 'That's all, your Worship, except that it's all lies what the officer says.'

MAGISTRATE: 'Is what you have said true, officer?'

POLICE OFFICER: 'Yes, your Worship. That's the case, your Worship.'

CLERK (To CORA): 'Now, do you wish to give evidence on oath or make a statement from where you are?'

CORA: 'I'll stay where I am, thank you. I was just waiting for a girlfriend. I didn't speak or look at anyone. The officer may have mistaken me for someone else. That man I was supposed to have spoken to, he spoke to me first. He asked me the time. I suppose he had an appointment and was late. That's why he hurried off. That's all I've got to say.'

The magistrate found the case proved and, on Cora admitting her previous convictions, which were read out, he ordered her to find two sureties for her good behaviour in the sum of twenty-five pounds each or go to prison for six months.

'It's a stinking shame,' shouted Cora before she was removed from the dock, to which she clung for a short time. 'Why don't you have your stinking name put up outside your stinking Court?'

Roger was rather disturbed by these cases. The Galahad in him became very prominent. Couldn't something be done for these girls? he asked himself. He wished he could help. He couldn't very well offer to be surety himself. For one thing he wasn't worth twenty-five pounds and for another he didn't think it would look well. But he made a mental resolution that if and when he had the power or opportunity, he would do all he could to help these wretched creatures, many of whom are born into the world without a reasonable chance. A morning at such a Court for a kind and thoughtful young man of twenty-one is a very moving experience. And so Roger found it. He must tell Sally.

The charges went on and Roger became even more worried at the speed with which they were disposed of and at the reliance the magistrate seemed to place on the evidence of the police. But after all, he said to himself, he ought to know. He's been there long enough. But how does he know a policeman's telling the truth and that the other chap isn't? I should find it jolly difficult sometimes. And just at that moment the magistrate dismissed a charge.

'Quite right to bring it, officer,' he said, 'but I think there's a doubt. You may go,' he said to the prisoner.

When Roger saw the smile on the prisoner's face as he left the Court he was not at all sure that his first fears were justified. But how difficult it must be to decide so many cases rightly. And so quickly. He decided to speak to Sally about that too. 'The tempo's too fast,' he would say. Her mother would appreciate that.

The charges were finished and the summonses began. They were all petty motoring offences.

'You're charged with leaving your motor car on such and such a day at such and such a place, so as to cause an obstruction. Are you Guilty or Not Guilty?'

'Guilty.'

'How long, officer?'

'One hour, thirty-five minutes.'

'Anything known?'

'Fined ten shillings for obstruction at Marlborough Street Magistrates' Court on 3rd June, 1947.'

'Anything to say?'

'I'm very sorry, but I didn't realize it was as long. There was nowhere else to leave it.'

'I know the difficulties, but they must be overcome or the streets would be impassable. Pay forty shillings, please.'

Then came a few pleas of Not Guilty.

The car hadn't been there as long as the officer said. It hadn't caused any obstruction. Why hadn't the officer taken the number of the other cars there? They were causing more obstruction. Some of the defendants were angry, some pained and some resigned to their fate, but they were all found guilty that day.

One lady who was fined said: 'I'd like you to know that I entirely disagree with your decision.'

'You can appeal, if you wish, madam.'

'I think you twisted what I said. It isn't fair.'

'That will be all, thank you, madam.' He might have been bowing her out of a shop. She tossed her head and left and Roger could imagine her telling all her friends of the grave injustice she had suffered at the hands of Mr

Meadowes. The fact remained that she had left her car in a busy street at a busy time of day when her car and any other vehicles which were left were bound to cause an obstruction. The fact also remained that she was fined no more than any of the others. But, of course, it was a grave injustice and the law is most unfair.

The summonses were finished and for once Roger did not feel alarmed as he did normally when the possibility of deputizing for Grimes drew near. The few kind remarks from the clerk made all the difference. Charles had told him of an experience he'd once had at a magistrate's court in the country. He had got to the Court early and he had had a long and pleasant talk with a man whom he believed to be the clerk to the justices. This gave Charles tremendous confidence, until the justices came in and he found that his friend was the usher and the clerk himself extremely fierce. Roger had made no such mistake. His friend was definitely the clerk.

'Well,' said Mr Meadowes, 'what are we waiting for?'

The clerk whispered to him: 'Grimes isn't here yet. There's only a youngster holding for him. D'you mind waiting a few minutes? He won't be any time. It's a heavy case.'

'All the more reason for getting on with it. Why can't he call the first witness? He can always be recalled if necessary. I won't let him be bounced. But we'll never get through these lists if we don't get on.'

'I rather told him you'd wait.'

'Well, now you'd better rather tell him I won't,' said Mr Meadowes. 'Cheer up,' he added. 'I shan't eat him, you know.'

'But I rather promised.'

'Well, this'll teach you not to. Never make promises myself. Bad habit. Thundering bad.'

The clerk thought he saw an opening.

'D'you think so, really? We sometimes get some of our clients to make promises and occasionally they keep them. That does a lot of good.'

'Well, you're not doing any,' said Mr Meadowes. 'I'm going to start this case, promises or no promises. Now, will you tell them to get on with it or shall I?'

The clerk looked apologetically at Roger and nodded to the jailer to bring in the prisoners. There was still no Mr Grimes. His solicitor rushed out to a telephone box.

'Where on earth is Mr Grimes?' he shouted down the mouthpiece.

'The senior's out, sir,' said a voice.

'I don't care where he is. Where's Mr Grimes? The case has been called on.'

'I'm afraid I don't know much about it, sir.'

'Give me patience,' said the solicitor.

At that moment a taxi drew up and out jumped Mr Grimes and Alec. The solicitor could see this from the telephone box and at once replaced the receiver. He rushed up to Grimes who was hurrying into the Court.

'The case has been called on,' he said excitedly.

'That's all right, my dear fellow,' said Mr Grimes. 'Here we are and now we shan't have to wait. So pleased to see ye, so pleased to see ye.'

And Mr Grimes dashed into the Court, panting more from habit than exertion, the distance from the taxi being much too short to put any real strain on the lungs. He slipped into counsel's row, bowed to the magistrate, whispered: 'Thank ye so much, my dear fellow,' to Roger and proceeded to address the magistrate.

'It's very good of your Worship to have waited,' he began.

'I didn't,' said Mr Meadowes. 'Too much to do.'

'If your Worship pleases,' said Mr Grimes and then opened the case to the magistrate. As Roger listened his admiration for Mr Grimes increased. He made everything crystal clear, every detail was in its right place, the story was unfolded efficiently, clearly and with overwhelming conviction. 'Will I ever be able to do it like that?' thought Roger. 'I can't believe it possible.'

As Henry had said, almost every pupil at the Bar thinks that his master does everything perfectly. Just as almost every juryman thinks a judge's summing up is brilliant. The point, of course, is, as Roger later learned, that, seldom having heard anything done professionally before, they have no standard to judge by. Mr Grimes' opening was certainly a perfectly proper, sound opening, but there was nothing spectacular about it and it was child's play to any experienced advocate who had mastered his facts.

The case went on for two hours and was adjourned for a week. It was some time before the hearing was completed, although the magistrate set aside several special days for it. Meantime, the men and women charged with the various crimes alleged had the prosecution hanging over their heads and some of them were in custody. That seemed to Roger rather hard on them if they were not guilty, though having heard what Mr Grimes had said about them, he could not conceive that any of them was innocent or would be acquitted. All the same, he thought, mightn't a few more magistrates and Courts be an advantage? He asked Henry about it.

'It's the Treasury,' said Henry. 'Of course it's their job to fight every bit of expenditure especially at this time when the country has been crippled by two wars and public expenditure is enormous. Every suggestion of an extra judge or extra magistrate is fought by them tooth and nail. But you mustn't forget they've got other claims on them from every quarter. They have to satisfy the most important. We naturally think the administration of justice is most important. But what about health and education? Are they less? Who's to judge? I can't. But of course, I agree that there ought to be extra magistrates. I shouldn't have thought anyone would have disagreed. But when you say it'll only cost so many thousands of pounds a year, that doesn't mean a thing until you add up all the other thousands of pounds you've got to spend and see where they're all to come from.'

CHAPTER EIGHTEEN

Brief Delivered

'I'd like you to meet Sally,' said Roger to Henry one day.

'I'd love to meet her,' said Henry. 'She sounds out of the ordinary.'

At that moment Alec came in.

'Thornton, Merivale want you to lead Mr Thursby in a bankruptcy matter, sir,' he said to Henry. 'Will that be all right?'

'Who are they?' said Henry. 'Never been to me before that I can remember.'

'They're clients of Mr Thursby, sir.'

'Oh, Uncle Alfred, of course,' said Henry. 'Well, that sounds very nice. Thank you, Alec.'

Alec went out and Henry turned to Roger.

'Is this your doing, old boy?' he asked.

'I know absolutely nothing about it,' he said. 'I'm as surprised as you are.'

'Oh, come now,' said Henry. 'You mustn't be surprised at someone sending me a brief. I do get them occasionally, you know. Even a new client sometimes puts his head in the door.'

'I'm sorry,' said Roger. 'I didn't mean it that way. But it's jolly lucky for me. I'm so glad you can take it. Will I be a nuisance? I know nothing about bankruptcy.'

'You'll learn,' said Henry. 'Particularly if you fail at the Bar. I wonder when it's for. Hope it doesn't clash with Ascot.'

'Are you a racing man, then?'

'Oh, gracious no, but there are such lovely things to be seen at Ascot, some with two legs and some with four, and the whole atmosphere appeals to me. It's the only meeting I go to. Like to come? If you've got any sense, you'll say "no." You stick to your work. You've a hell of a lot to learn. But I'll take you if you want – and Sally too, if you'd like.'

'I think that's most unfair,' said Roger. 'Why did you have to ask me – and Sally? You know I'd love it. I hope the bankruptcy case prevents it. Anyway, what would Grimes say?'

'Grimes? He'd say, "Dear, dear, dear, going to Ascot are we? Going to the races instead of getting on with our work, are we? Dear, dear, dear. Have a good time, my dear fellow, have a good time. Goodbye, bye, bye." '

'Well, I shall consult Sally on the subject,' said Roger. As he said that, the junior clerk came into the room and said that Roger was wanted on the telephone by a Miss Burnett. He went to the telephone.

'Hullo, Joy,' said Roger.

'Oh, Roger, Uncle Alfred told me he was sending you another brief – and I just wondered if you'd got it.'

'Oh, yes, Joy. I don't know if it's come yet, but I've just this moment heard about it.'

Joy was in her uncle's office at the time and it had all been arranged in her presence so that it was not exactly a coincidence that she telephoned when she did. She believed in striking while the iron was hot and she thought that Roger had a conscience.

'I'm so pleased for you,' said Joy. 'You are doing well. It seems ages since I saw you. I was wondering – ' and she paused to give Roger an opportunity to do what any decent man, who'd had a brief from a girl, would do.

'So was I,' said Roger, with as much enthusiasm as he could muster. 'I'd love to take you out one night soon if you're free.'

'Any night, Roger. I'd put anything else off if it clashed.' At that moment there was a knock on the clerks' door. The junior opened the door and in came Sally. Roger was just saying: 'Well, let me see, how would tomorrow do?' when he noticed her.

Sally had a brief in her hand.

'That would be lovely, Roger. Where and when?'

'Oh,' said Roger most uncomfortably. 'Anywhere at all.'

'Will you call for me, then?'

'Yes, certainly.'

'About seven?'

'Yes.'

'You sound awfully distrait all of a sudden. Is it another client?'

'I'd like to think so,' said Roger.

'How lovely,' said Joy, 'if it is.'

A remark which embarrassed Roger very much indeed. He managed to finish the conversation with Joy and then turned to find Sally talking to the clerk.

'I've brought these papers down for Mr Blagrove,' she was saying. 'Mr Sharpe would be glad if he could have them back quickly. Hullo, Roger.'

'What on earth are you doing here?'

'My people have just sent a brief down to Mr Blagrove. No one else was available, so they asked me to bring it. Funny, isn't it?'

'I didn't know you did any litigation.'

'Oh, the firm does, but not the partner I work for. But this is from him. It's an opinion about a landlord and tenant matter. Mr Sharpe thought he'd like to try your Mr Blagrove. Have *you* had any more briefs lately?'

'I have, as a matter of fact.'

'From the same source?'

Roger blushed. He could not help it. 'Yes, if you want to know, but we oughtn't to chat here. It'll disturb the clerks. Come in and meet Henry.'

'Won't I be taking up too much of your time? Briefs and telephone conversations and things,' she added.

'Henry would love to meet you. Do come in.'

He took her to Henry's room and introduced them. 'I've heard so much about you,' said Sally, 'though you're not quite what I expected. That isn't meant to be rude. On the contrary, as a matter of fact.'

'Well, you're exactly what I expected, and knowing the source of my information, you couldn't ask for more than that, could you?' said Henry.

'I should like to think that,' said Sally. 'So this is where you decide how not to ask leading questions and whether to put the prisoner in the box and if the judge is likely to be prejudiced if you plead the Statute of Limitations?'

'You seem to know an awful lot about it,' said Henry.

'I've been with solicitors for three months. I've brought you a brief.'

'Me – you mean Roger.'

'I don't, my firm's pretty careful who it briefs. I hope I shan't have my neck wrung for suggesting you. It'll be Roger's fault. But he thinks you've the wisdom of a Lord Chief Justice and the power of advocacy of a Carson and he's managed to put it across to me. He doesn't always succeed.'

'Well, I hope it's something I can do. Your neck would be very much on my conscience. I'll certainly give it more than usual attention. Dispatch will oblige, I suppose!'

'Expedition specially requested,' said Sally 'is the form we use in our office when the papers have been overlooked for a week and the client is howling for that opinion we promised him.'

'Well – I've nothing to do – so – oh, yes, I have, though. Roger's getting me all my work.'

'I see,' said Sally. 'How nice. Does he get a commission? Or give one perhaps? Now I must go or I'll be shot. We've a lot to do in my office. Goodbye, so glad to have met you at last. Goodbye, Roger. We must meet some time out of working hours – if you have a spare moment.'

The truth of the matter was that for quite a little time Roger had been neglecting both Joy and Sally. He had been devoting himself almost entirely to work. Now he found it a little disconcerting to be subjected to this two-pronged attack. He saw Sally out and went back to Henry.

'Roger,' said Henry, 'if at any time you should commit yourself irrevocably to Uncle Alfred's niece, would you consider it a breach of good faith if I asked your friend Sally out to dinner?'

CHAPTER NINETEEN

The Old Bailey

In due course the conspiracy case came on for trial at the Old Bailey. It was likely to take a fortnight or three weeks and in consequence to interfere a good deal with Mr Grimes' other work. Roger had considerable qualms. He felt sure he would be left to do part of it. Peter, on the other hand, would have been delighted to be left with it. It was his ambition to stand up at the Old Bailey and say something, and he had the doubtful advantage that he would never realize how badly he had said it. He said to Roger that, if Grimeyboy went away in the middle, he thought that, as he was senior to Roger, he ought to have the chance of taking over before him.

'Of course,' said Roger and hoped that was how it would be.

'Since you came here,' said Peter, 'he hardly ever seems to use me. I don't think he likes me somehow.'

I wonder if that is it, thought Roger, or if I really am better. It was an interesting day for Roger when he went for the first time to the Old Bailey. He was surprised at the smallness of the Courts. But the solemnity was there all right. He tried to visualize the murderers and other criminals who had stood in the dock. This was the Court in which, Henry had told him, five blackmailers had once stood to receive their sentences from the then Lord Chief Justice. The Lord Chief Justice awarded the first man he sentenced eight years penal servitude (as it was then called), the second ten years, the third twelve. It must have been obvious to the fifth man, the ringleader, what the judge was working up to, and slowly and methodically he worked up to it.

'And as this is the worst case of its kind I have ever tried,' he began in sentencing the ringleader, 'the sentence of the Court is that you be kept in penal servitude for life.'

'I'm told,' Henry had said, 'that it was an artistic, though not a pleasant performance.'

This, too, was the Court where the man who was said to have been a sort of Jekyll and Hyde had stood to receive his sentence.

'Counsel has argued eloquently on your behalf,' said the judge, 'that you are really two people, one very good and the other very bad. As to that, all I can say is that both of you must go to prison.'

Roger would have been spared some unnecessary worry if he had known that Mr Grimes had given his personal undertaking to be present the whole time throughout the case, and Alec had charged a fee to compensate for the results of complying with such an undertaking. Mr Grimes was there all the time, and Roger had the advantage of seeing him hold innumerable conferences on other matters with solicitors and managing clerks in the corridors of the Old Bailey. In the middle of a case involving theft of machinery, he discussed among other things a libel action brought by a politician, a claim for damages for being caught up in a sausage machine, an action by a householder against his next-door neighbour for nuisance by barking dogs, a claim for breach of contract on the sale of fertilizers, an action for breach of promise, some bankruptcy proceedings, an appeal to the Privy Council and a host of other things. A temperamental recording machine which decided not to record from time to time would have produced some surprising results if it had been placed by the side of Mr Grimes eating a sandwich on a bench in the Old Bailey, while client after client came and told his tale of woe, received expert advice and went away rejoicing. And Mr Grimes never put a foot wrong. A lesser man might have confused one case with another. But not he. Mr Grimes treated each client as though he were his only client and as though his case were his only case.

'Yes, my dear fellow. Don't ye worry, my dear fellow, that's quite all right. Just write and tell them the tale, my dear fellow. Goodbye, bye, bye.'

'Dear, dear, dear. You don't say, my dear fellow, dear, dear, dear, you don't say. Well, we'll soon put a stop to those goings on. Ye wait, my dear fellow, ye'll see. It'll be quite all right, quite all right. Goodbye, bye, bye.' And so on and so on, punctuated by bites of sandwich. Do this, don't do that, try for this but take that if necessary, apply to the judge, go to the Master, issue a writ, pay into Court, appeal, don't appeal, it's a toss up, my dear fellow, we can but try; dear, dear, dear, they will do these things, my dear fellow, they will do these things.

And so back into Court, stomach full of ill-bitten, undigested sandwich, head, Roger would have thought, full of dogs, sausages and fertilizers – but not at all. Mr Grimes examined a difficult witness as though he had been doing nothing else but think about his evidence. Roger was astonished at the number of watertight compartments there must be in a busy barrister's mind. But then, I suppose, he said to himself, it's exactly the same with everyone's job. I don't imagine a surgeon often takes out the wrong part because he's confused two cases or that a doctor, visiting a case of measles, enquires about the big toe, which belongs next door.

The case went on day after day. Roger took voluminous notes, Peter took a few, and from time to time when he found that his services were not going to be required, wandered into the other Courts where something more interesting might be happening. Once while Peter was away, the judge said: 'Excuse me a moment, Mr Grimes. A prisoner wants a dock defence.'

'Put up Arthur Green,' said the clerk and Mr Green was brought up into the dock.

'You may choose whom you wish,' said the judge.

'That one, please, my Lord,' said Mr Green, and pointed to Mr Grimes.

'I'm afraid Mr Grimes is engaged on a case,' said the judge.

'I thought you said I could choose whom I wish, my Lord,' said Mr Green. 'I want him.'

'I'm sorry,' said the judge. 'Mr Grimes can't be in two Courts at once.'

'I don't want him in two Courts at once, my Lord,' said Mr Green. 'Just in mine.'

'Now, don't waste time,' said the judge. 'You can't have him, though no doubt Mr Grimes is suitably flattered. Now, choose someone else.'

'Oh, well, I'll have him,' and Mr Green pointed to counsel defending the chief conspirator.

'I'm sorry,' said the judge. 'He's engaged too.'

'I thought you said – ' began the man.

'I know, I know,' said the judge. 'But you can't have someone who's engaged on a case.'

'How am I to know who's engaged on a case and who isn't, my Lord? Perhaps you could ask the gentlemen who aren't for hire to cover up their flags, my Lord.'

'Now, don't be impertinent,' said the judge quite genially. 'I'm sorry about this. Perhaps those members of the Bar who are not engaged in the case would be good enough to stand up.'

Three old, three middle-aged and three young men sprang to their feet with alacrity. This was a race in which youth had no advantage over age. Indeed a middle-aged man was first, though he ricked his back in the process. Roger remained seated.

'Get up, my dear fellow,' said Mr Grimes. 'Ye never know. Good experience for ye.'

So Roger got up a little time after the others, just as Mr Green had come to much the same conclusion as the old lag in Henry's story. The apparent reluctance which Roger had to join the race appealed to Mr Green.

'Him, my Lord, please,' said Mr Green, pointing to Roger.

'Mr – Mr – ' began the judge, and then made a noise, half grunt, half swallow, three consonants and a couple of vowels. It was a work of art and had been cultivated by him over the years. It really sounded like a name and though no one could say what it was, no one could say what it was not. Whether a name began with a vowel or a consonant or a diphthong, the sound made by the judge was not unlike it, and, as he looked hard at its owner during the process, it never failed.

'Will you undertake this defence, please?' said the judge.

'If your Lordship pleases.'

Roger wondered what was the next move.

'Go and see him,' volunteered his next-door neighbour.

'Now?' asked Roger.

'Of course.'

'Where do I see him?'

'In the cells. Bow to the judge and go into the dock and down the stairs. Quick. The old boy's waiting for you.'

Roger looked up and saw that his informant was right. 'Don't disturb yourself unduly,' said the judge. 'This case is going to last for weeks, anyway. What difference does an extra half hour make?'

Roger blushed. 'I'm so sorry, my Lord,' he said.

The judge gave him a friendly smile.

Roger walked into the dock rather self-consciously and went down the stairs which led from inside it to the cells below. He was shown to a room in which he could interview Mr Green who was promptly brought to him.

'Afternoon, sir,' said Mr Green.

'Good afternoon,' said Roger.

'Funny weather for the time of year,' said Mr Green. 'Felt like thunder this morning.'

'Yes, it did,' said Roger.

'But there,' said Mr Green, 'they will do these things.'

'What!' said Roger.

'He defended me twenty years ago,' said Mr Green. 'I haven't forgotten. Nearly got me off too. If it hadn't been for the old judge he would have too. Dear, dear, dear. Now we're starting to look back. And that won't do. We must look forward, mustn't we? This your first case?'

'Not quite,' said Roger.

'That's all right,' said Mr Green. 'I'll tell you what to do. It's easy, dead easy. I'd have done it myself but it looks better to have a mouthpiece. Can you sing?' he added.

'I don't know quite what that's got to do with it,' said Roger.

'Ah!' said Mr Green knowingly, 'but you haven't been at it as long as I have. There's a lot of things you don't understand now, aren't there?'

'Yes,' said Roger. 'I'm afraid there are.'

'Well, now that's agreed – can you sing?'

'No, I can't, as a matter of fact.'

'Never mind,' said Mr Green. 'As long as I know one way or the other. Can't take any chances. Forewarned is forearmed. Many a mickle makes a muckle. It's an ill wind and so on and so forth. I'm not keeping you, I hope?'

'I'm here to defend you,' said Roger. 'My time's your time. My services, such as they are, are at your disposal.'

'That's a pretty speech,' said Mr Green. 'Can you make lots of those?'

Roger did not answer.

'All right,' said Mr Green. 'You win. Cut the cackle and come to the hosses. Now, I'll tell you what we'll do. I've got it all laid on.'

'But what are you charged with?' asked Roger.

'Oh, that!' said Mr Green scornfully. 'It's almost an insult. But I suppose it's like everything else these days. Going down. You've only got to deration butter and all the places serve margarine.'

'I don't understand,' said Roger.

'Now, look,' said Mr Green. 'Have you ever seen an indictment before?'

Roger had not and said so. He would have admitted it anyway, but he made the admission a second before he realized that it was a pretty odd system under which a young man who had never seen an indictment could be employed to defend somebody who was charged upon one. Roger had read the charges in Mr Grimes' conspiracy case, but for some reason he had never actually seen the indictment or a copy of it.

'Well, now, look – this is an indictment – or it's supposed to be.'

He produced a typewritten foolscap document. All over it were pencil remarks made by himself.

'I call it an impertinence,' went on Mr Green. 'Do you know that I was once charged on an indictment containing thirty-three counts? Thirty-three. Now that's not bad, eh?'

'What happened?' asked Roger.

'Never mind what happened. That's not the point. But it's treating a chap with respect to bring in thirty-three counts. Shows you're frightened you might miss him here and there. Can't afford to take chances with him. I've had twenty-five, twenty and never less than ten or twelve. Oh, yes, I once had seven. And now look at this – I ask you – is it fair? Is it reasonable? I'm not so young as I was, I'm entitled to a bit of respect, aren't I? One count – one solitary, miserable count. They must think I've come down in the world. It hurts. That's what it does. If you've got a nice lot of counts to deal with, you've got something to fight. But this – this – it takes all the stuffing out of a man. I tell you – I had a good mind to plead Guilty and be done with it. One count! Two can play at that game. If they won't do the right thing, why should I? I've never pleaded Guilty in my life, but I tell you, I came as near doing it this time as I ever did. And then I remembered it was Ascot next week. So that wouldn't do. But if it hadn't been, I tell you – I'd have cut the ground from under their feet. Guilty, I should have said. That would have shaken them. There they are – counsel, solicitors, police, witnesses, judge, jury, ushers, flowers, herbs, spectators – everyone – and I say Guilty. I bet the clerk wouldn't have believed it. What was that? he'd have said. I'd have had a game with him. Not Guilty, I should have said. Oh, I thought you said Guilty, he'd have said. Yes, I'd have said, I did. Well, which is it, he'd have said, Guilty or Not Guilty. You choose, I should have said. I hate these parlour games. One of these days a judge will say – they look at TV all right, oh, yes they do, whatever they say – one of these days a judge will say – will the next prisoner sign in, please?'

'Now, look, Mr Green,' said Roger. 'I know I'm very new to the Bar, but you're paying me to help you. Hadn't you better tell me about the case? I love to hear your views on these other matters, but after all, if you want to go to Ascot next week the case is more important.'

'You'll do well, sir,' said Mr Green. 'You think of essentials. Ascot it is. I've never missed an Ascot yet – except when – well now I'm going back into past history. Dear, dear, dear. Now, let's get down to brass tacks. No beating about the bush. All fair and above board. In for a penny, in for a pound. Who laughs last, laughs loudest. You can't sing, I think you said?'

'Mr Green,' said Roger, 'this is a little difficult to say and please don't think I'm meaning to be offensive, but have you ever thought of pleading – that is – I mean – I hope you'll understand – putting up a defence of – of – insanity?'

'Cheer up,' said Mr Green. 'I always do this to begin with. Don't let it get you down. Helps me find out what sort of a chap you are. Now look. There's only one count against me. There's nothing in it at all. We're as good as out in the road already – only we're not. But don't you worry, we shall be. Now, d'you see what it says here?'

He showed Roger the indictment.

'Obtaining money by false pretences with intent to defraud. Well, it's ridiculous, that's what it is. It's laughable. It won't stick. They'll never wear it. Are you agreed upon your verdict? We are. Do you find the prisoner Arthur Green Guilty or Not Guilty. Not Guilty. Not Guilty, and is that the verdict of you all? It is. And out we go. Shame I couldn't get bail or I wouldn't have been inside at all.'

'Really,' said Roger. 'Time's getting on. You must tell me the facts. Have you a copy of the depositions?'

'That's a fair question. And here's a fair answer. Yes.'

'Can I see them, please?'

'Don't you think they might put you off?'

'Mr Green, if you're not mad and want me to defend you, you must let me see the depositions.'

'At last,' said Mr Green. 'Say it louder next time. I'm not sorry I chose you, but you're making me work. Don't you understand, young man, that at your game you've got to be able to shout down the other side, the judge, the jury and all? And what hope have you got if you can't shout me down? Eh? None at all. It's taken me ten minutes to get you annoyed even. Come on, get tough, let's see some rough stuff. Tear 'em to pieces.'

'All right,' said Roger. 'P'raps you'd tell me what it's all about in as few words as possible, please.'

'Apart from the "please" that was all right. Good. I'll tell you. It's simple as pie. I'm charged with obtaining money by false pretences. How much money? Twenty pounds. A beggarly twenty pounds. How did I get it? By selling toffee. That's right, toffee. I get the money, they get the toffee. What's wrong with that?'

'Nothing as far as I can see – if they get enough toffee.'

'That's quick of you. Enough toffee. Well, as a matter of fact, they didn't, but they're not charging me with that. Look – you see – all it says is "by falsely pretending that a letter signed G St Clair Smith was a genuine reference when in fact it was written by the accused himself." That's all, positively all. It's laughable.'

184

'Well – there is a Mr St Clair Smith then and he wrote it?'

'Be reasonable,' said Mr Green. 'Fair's fair and all that. But how would I get as far as this if there was a Mr Smith – St Clair or not?'

'Then there isn't anyone?'

'No idea. There may be for all I know,' said Mr Green.

'Then who wrote the reference?'

'Who do you think?'

'Well,' said Roger, 'if you ask me to be frank, I think you did.'

'Don't be bashful about it,' said Mr Green. 'Of course I did. Who else could have done – except Mr Smith, of course, and we're not sure about him, are we?'

'Well,' said Roger, 'if you wrote yourself a reference and pretended that it was written by Mr Smith, what's your defence?'

'They had the toffee, of course.'

'But not enough?'

'They don't complain that it wasn't enough here. They just say about the reference.'

'Yes, I see,' said Roger. 'But you had twenty pounds from them, didn't you?'

'Certainly.'

'How much toffee did they get?'

'At least a quarter of what they ordered. More like a third.'

'But you got the full price?'

'That's right.'

'Well, I'm bound to say it sounds pretty fishy to me,' said Roger.

'Of course it does. If it didn't sound fishy, I shouldn't be here, should I? I'll tell you something else. It was fishy. But that doesn't mean it was a crime. Oh, dear, no. It's a postal

185

business I run. Cash with order, I say. Fair enough? And in my first letter I always offer a reference. What's more, I give them a reference whether they want it or not.'

'You mean,' said Roger, 'you write yourself a reference under another name?'

'I mean,' said Mr Green, 'precisely that. But this chap, like most of them, has too sweet a tooth, that's his trouble. He wants his toffee. So he doesn't bother about a reference and just sends his money.'

'Then I can't see why on earth you're charged if that's the only false pretence alleged. They've got to prove they relied on it and if they hadn't had it they couldn't have relied on it.'

'Smart boy,' said Mr Green. 'You saw the point.'

'Yes,' said Roger. 'But you did send a reference.'

'You bet I did,' said Mr Green. 'I always do.'

'And he must have had it before he sent the money,' said Roger, 'or the case wouldn't have gone on like this. You must let me see the depositions.'

'All right,' said Mr Green. 'As you are so pressing,' and he handed them to Roger, who read them for a few minutes.

'Well, it's quite plain from these that he had the reference first,' said Roger. 'I knew he must have done.'

'Well, he didn't,' said Mr Green. 'The quickness of the hand deceives the eye. I can prove be didn't.'

'How?'

'Elementary, my dear – I beg your pardon, sir. I shouldn't have done that. But it is too, too simple. Shall I explain?'

'Please do,' said Roger.

'How d'you catch mice?' said Mr Green.

'Now really – ' began Roger.

'With bait,' went on Mr Green. 'I send my little reference on the 24th but I actually date it the 20th. What happens?

Complaints are made by the public about my toffee. Not enough of it. Stale, bad, rotten toffee, and so on. Now, for one reason or another I didn't want the police prying into my affairs, looking at my books (if any), and so on and so forth. So, after I've had the money, I send this nice little reference in pretty obviously disguised handwriting. Aha, say they, we've got him. Handwriting experts and all that. His handwriting. And the date? Just before the customer sent the money. We've got him, they say. The customer doesn't want much persuading that he had the reference before he sent the money, particularly when the police point out the date. "You must have done," they say. "So I must," says he. So they don't bother to look into my affairs except quite casually. A false reference is good enough for them. Saves them a lot of trouble. He's in the bag, they say. But, you see, he isn't. That's just where he isn't. Proof of posting isn't proof of delivery, eh? But it's proof of *non-*delivery. I get a receipt for my letter. And here it is. Shows I sent the letter after he sent the money. I tell you he had too sweet a tooth. They all have. Of course, when they come and see me and show me Mr St Clair Smith's letter I pretend I haven't seen it before, but I look nice and uncomfortable when I say it and what with the date on it, my other letter and the handwriting expert, they're happy as sandboys.

' "Did you believe it to be a genuine reference, Mr Sweet Tooth?"

' "I did."

' "If you had not believed it was a genuine reference, would you have sent the money?"

' "I would not."

' "Thank you, Mr Sweet Tooth." '

'Are you sure,' said Roger, 'that you only sent one letter to him at about that time?'

'Ah,' said Mr Green. 'I'm not so bad at choosing counsel after all. And you're not such a – now what am I saying? That's the one question you've got to ask. "Did you have any letter from the defendant?" I prefer that to "prisoner," but I don't really mind if you forget – "did you have any letter from the defendant at about the time you received the reference?" Well, he'll have to say "no" – but that's the one point you've got to be careful of. Once you've held him down to that, we're home. Out comes the receipt for posting and I can go and lose all the money I haven't paid you at Ascot. Right?'

'I see the point,' said Roger. 'I must think about it.'

Later that day when Roger returned to the Temple after completing his conference with Mr Green, he consulted Henry on the matter.

'You can never tell,' said Henry. 'If the chap admits that no other letters were sent to him at that time it looks like a winner. But don't you be too sure about getting that admission. And if you get the admission don't go on pressing him about it. That's a mistake beginners often make. They get the admission they need and they're so pleased about it they go on asking questions about it and before they know where they are, if the witness hasn't actually withdrawn the admission, he's what you might call blurred it, by adding words like, "Well, I'm not quite sure" or "perhaps I'm wrong" and "now I come to think of it there may have been another letter." Economy in cross-examination is very necessary.'

'Thanks very much,' said Roger. 'Yes, I see. I am grateful. Now, another thing. It won't arise in this case because I haven't any witnesses except the prisoner. But I always thought counsel wasn't supposed to see witnesses and I saw one or two counsel with a lot of people round them.

I didn't hear what they were saying, but I should have thought some of them probably were witnesses.'

'Well,' said Henry, 'a good deal of latitude is allowed to counsel for the defence in criminal cases, but you're quite right in thinking that, generally speaking, counsel shouldn't talk to the witnesses except his own client or expert witnesses. But it's a matter for counsel's discretion, and in an exceptional case he certainly can. But don't you try to pretend to yourself that a case is exceptional when it isn't. We don't want you to get like old Ian McTavish, though I'm sure you won't.'

'Who was he?'

'He was a lovable old man, whom everyone liked, but he was an old rascal. The story goes that his opponent in a fraud case at a County Court found the old boy in the consultation-room surrounded by witnesses, saying: "Now then, boys, all together. 'We relied upon the representations.' " '

CHAPTER TWENTY

Dock Brief

Roger had a difficult decision to make the day before the case of Mr Green came on for trial at the Old Bailey. Should he ask Sally, Joy and his mother, or alternatively one or more and which of them? He would dearly have liked his triumph – if it was to be one – witnessed, but on the other hand, suppose things went wrong and he made a fool of himself again? Eventually he decided to ask Sally her opinion.

'Roger,' she said, 'I should love to hear you, I really should. But d'you know, if I were you, I should wait until you've got more confidence. It's always possible the thought of one of us – never mind which – will distract or worry you. Then again – you might actually start to act for our benefit and that would be really bad. I'm doing myself out of a lot in saying this, because I'm sure my Mr Sharpe would let me go if I wanted to.'

'*Our* Mr Sharpe?'

'Roger,' said Sally, 'you're not jealous?'

'Of course not,' said Roger.

'No, I was afraid I must be mistaken.'

'Surely you don't want me to be jealous?'

'Oh, Roger, you are young. Never mind. Forget it. Will you ask Joy to go to the Old Bailey?'

'Of course not,' said Roger. 'I nearly always take your advice. I've never known you wrong yet.'

'Dear Roger, you're so sweet – and unformed.'

'You think I'm an awful ass.'

'I don't think anything of the sort. F E Smith was unformed once and all the others. You've lots of time. And d'you know – I think you've come on, even in the last six months.'

'Do you really? You're not just trying to be nice?'

'Have you ever known me? No, I'd really like to come to the Old Bailey to see the difference. I'm sure it'll be considerable.'

'Do come, Sally – I'd love you to be there.'

'Don't tempt me, Roger. It isn't fair. You tell me all about it when it's over.'

That evening Roger had an appointment to dine with Mr Merivale.

'My dear Roger,' said Mr Merivale. 'How very nice to see you. Very good of you to give me the time. You won't be able to go out in the evenings much longer. Nose to the grindstone, my boy. But that's the Bar. Either too much work or too little. How are things going?'

'As a matter of fact,' said Roger, 'I've got a brief at the Old Bailey tomorrow.'

'Dear me,' said Mr Merivale. 'For the prosecution or defence?'

'Defence.'

'Pleading Guilty?'

'Oh, no. I hope to get him off.'

'That's the way, my boy. Be a fighter. Ah, here's Joy. She'll have to give me a report on you. In case we have any big criminal cases.'

'Oh, what's all this?' said Joy.

'I've got a case at the Old Bailey tomorrow.'

'Oh, how lovely,' said Joy.

'And you're going to report it for me,' said Mr Merivale. 'I shall send you both in my car.'

'Oh, uncle – you are sweet,' said Joy and gave him a kiss.

'It's most kind of you,' said Roger, who did not see how he could possibly get out of it.

Roger did not tell his mother about the case. He decided to wait until it was over. It would be more effective and she'd be more likely to listen. On the day before the trial she was particularly difficult.

'Oh dear, oh dear,' she kept on saying. 'I'll forget my own name next.'

Roger was quite used to this sort of thing, but he asked politely: 'What is it, Mother darling?'

'If I knew, my pet, would I be asking? But there's something I've forgotten that I've got to do. And terrible things will happen if I don't do it.'

'What terrible things?'

'My dear, darling Roger, how should I know until they happen? Then it'll be too late. Of course if I could think what it was I had to do, they wouldn't happen. Be an angel and think for me. You know I don't do it very well.'

'I expect you've got to do something for Aunt Ethel.'

'No, I think it's more important than Aunt Ethel.'

'It must be serious then,' said Roger. 'I've got something important to do tomorrow too, but I'll tell you that later.'

'Another examination, Roger darling? Surely not?'

'Now Mother, really! You know I'm qualified. You've seen me in Court.'

'But you could still have examinations. Doctors do. The one who helped me with you said he wanted to be a gynaecologist. I was very flattered.'

The next day Mr Merivale sent Joy in his car to fetch Roger and take them both to the Temple and thence to the Old Bailey.

'Oh, Roger, I'm so excited,' said Joy. 'Now you really are starting. I'm sure no one as young as you has ever had a case at the Old Bailey. Oh, Roger – I do love you – and you do love me, don't you, Roger? It's at times like these when I feel it so terribly.'

She squeezed his hand. He squeezed hers.

'If I don't sound very affectionate, Joy, it's because I'm thinking about the case. A man may go to prison because of me – or be free because of me. It's a dreadful responsibility.'

'I'm so proud of you, Roger,' whispered Joy.

That morning Mr Sharpe sent for Sally.

'Sally,' he said, 'I wonder if you'd do me a small favour?'

'Of course,' said Sally.

'There's a young man I know – or know of, I should say,' he began.

'No, thank you,' said Sally. 'It's very kind of you all the same.'

'Now, how on earth d'you know what I'm going to say? I know a lot of young men – a very large number. I go to a boys' club among other things.'

'I hope none of them are where you're about to suggest I should go.'

Sally had told Mr Sharpe some days previously about Roger's case.

'Well, sorry,' said Mr Sharpe, 'if it can't be *volens*, it'll have to be *nolens volens*. As your study of the law of contract will have told you, an employee is bound to obey all reasonable orders of his or her employer.'

'Very good, sir,' said Sally.

'You will proceed,' said Mr Sharpe, 'to the Old Bailey with all convenient haste. You will there make enquiry as to where a gentleman called Arthur Green is being tried and you will go to that Court, mentioning my name if necessary, in order to get you in – and bring me a complete report of the case. Go along now. You know you're dying to.'

'But it won't be fair,' said Sally. 'I've stopped him taking Joy.'

'Good thing too,' said Mr Sharpe. 'I never did like the sound of that girl. You know the motto. Anyway, you can't help yourself, you're under orders. Get the sack if you don't. Then who'll give you your articles?'

'What was that?' said Sally.

'I said it,' said Mr Sharpe.

'Oh, oh – ' said Sally about as excited as Roger had been when she told him he was going to be a great man. 'Oh – oh – I could kiss you.'

'I'm afraid,' said Mr Sharpe, 'that my wife would not approve of that even from a brunette. Pity. I should have liked the experience.'

'You are good. Why are you so nice to me?' said Sally.

'I'm not particularly nice to you. I like people as a whole. As for you – I think you've got more brains for a girl of twenty-one than I've ever heard of. You'll end up President of the Law Society – unless you go and get married or something. And even then – which reminds me – I believe I've just given you a job of work. Off with you. And a full report, mind you – not only the mistakes.'

Before he went to Court Roger had a final word with Henry while Joy stayed in the car.

'It's quite definite, isn't it, that I only get one speech,' Roger said, 'and that's after I've called the prisoner?'

'Quite definite,' said Henry, 'and make it a good one.'

194

Roger rejoined Joy and they drove to the Old Bailey, almost in silence, Roger becoming more and more nervous, like a runner before a race. They arrived at the Court and he took Joy through the main entrance. He decided to show her into Court before he robed. Ordinary spectators are supposed to go to the public gallery, but members of the legal profession can usually obtain admission for their friends to the body of the Court, unless the event is a very popular one. But the attendant at the entrance to the Court checks and sometimes stops the people who enter or try to do so.

'What do you want?' he asked politely but suspiciously of Roger.

'I'm Counsel,' said Roger with as much assurance as he could manage.

'Oh,' said the man, plainly taken aback. 'I'm sorry, sir. I didn't – ' He didn't finish the sentence.

Roger showed Joy in and then went up to the robing-room. When he came back to the Court it was twenty past ten. His case was first in the list. Nearly zero hour. As he came into the Court a police officer came up to him.

'Are you Mr Thursby by any chance?' he asked.

Roger said he was.

'Your client wants to see you at once, sir,' he said.

He went hurriedly into the dock and down the stairs, wondering what it could be. Had he been more experienced he would not have been in the least surprised. Later he found out that old offenders, particularly those charged with fraud, often ask to see their counsel before and during the case and send them voluminous notes throughout the hearing. They are usually irrelevant and nearly always repetitive.

'Good morning,' said Mr Green. 'I hope you slept well.'

'What is it?' said Roger. 'There's only a few minutes before the case starts.'

'Now, don't get fidgety,' said Mr Green. 'When you've done this as often as I have you'll be quite calm and steady. Look at me. My teeth aren't chattering, are they?'

'No.'

'I'm not shaking like a leaf, am I?'

'No,' said Roger, irritable with nervousness.

'Now would you not say that I was in very good shape?' asked Mr Green.

'What has this got to do with it?' said Roger. 'I thought you wanted to see me about the case.'

'Look,' said Mr Green, 'you're my counsel aren't you?'

'Yes.'

'Well, I can ask my counsel questions, can't I?'

'Yes.'

'Well, I'm asking one. Would you consider that I was in very good shape? It's important, you know. If you thought I wasn't, you might want an adjournment. It's I who've got to go in the witness box and lie like a trooper, not you.'

'But you're not going to commit perjury?' said Roger, anxiously.

'Just a manner of speaking,' said Mr Green. 'I shall tell them much more truth than I gave them toffee. Now, how am I? Is my tie straight?'

'Really!' said Roger, and then said very seriously: 'You will tell the truth, won't you?'

'What d'you take me for?' said Mr Green. 'Anyone would think I was a crook. You'll hurt my feelings if you're not careful. And then where shall we be? Now, what about the tie? Does it cover the stud all right?'

'This is ridiculous,' said Roger.

'Come, come, sir,' said Mr Green. 'I'm playing the leading part in this show. You may think you are till it comes to going to jail. Then you'll cheerfully yield pride of place to me. True, isn't it? You wouldn't go to jail instead of me, would you?'

'No,' said Roger.

'Right, then, I'm the leading actor, and you don't send him on to the stage looking anyhow. He has a dresser, doesn't he? Couldn't afford one as well as you. So I thought you wouldn't mind giving me the once-over. Hair all right?'

'Quite,' said Roger. That was easy. There was none.

'Trouser creases all right?'

'Very good.'

'Pity I haven't got that gold tooth. I flogged it during my last stretch. Got some jam for it. D'you like jam?'

'I'm going back into Court,' said Roger, 'or I shan't be there when the judge comes in.'

'Don't be cross,' said Mr Green. 'You'll never do any good if you're cross. Give me a nice smile. Come on. That's better. Now take it easy. It's going to be perfectly all right. Next time I see you it won't be here. Won't be at Ascot, I'm afraid. Can't get into the Royal Enclosure any more. Even Mr St Clair Smith couldn't get me in.'

At that moment a warder came into the room.

'The judge is just going to sit, sir,' he said.

'Good luck,' said Mr Green. 'Chin up, head high, no heel taps, all's fair in love and war, dark the dawn when day is nigh, faint heart never won – oh – he's gone.' He turned to the warder: 'I almost threw that one back,' he said, 'but you should have seen the one that got away.'

Roger only just had time to get into the Court before the knocks heralding the arrival of the judge. The judge took his seat, and Roger, having bowed low, sat down and looked across at the jury who were to try Mr Green. As he did so two ladies came into Court and were shown to the seats behind counsel. But for the sight which met his eyes Roger might have noticed them. They were Sally and her mother. They had met outside the Court.

'What on earth are you doing, Mother?' Sally had said.

'Well, I thought, as you weren't going, I would. Now I see that I might have done some more practising. Well, as I'm here I might as well stay. Which way do we go in? I promise not to sing.'

The sight which had so shaken Roger was that of his mother sitting in the front row of the jury. At the last moment she had remembered what it was she had had to do. She sat cheerfully in the jury box looking interestedly at everything in the Court. Her eye travelled from the judge to the seats for counsel.

'That one looks a bit young,' she said to herself as she looked along the line. 'Quite like Roger really. Yes, very. I must tell him. Quite a striking likeness. Good gracious, it is Roger. Well, really, he might have told me. I wonder if he'll speak. Should I smile at him or won't he like it? Why shouldn't I? After all, I'm his mother.'

She beamed at her son, and waved her hand slightly.

Roger went red in the face. He adored his mother and hated to hurt her feelings, but it was very difficult to smile. And, of course, he couldn't wave. He turned round to see if people had noticed his mother waving to him. On his right was Joy where he had put her. On his left were Sally and her mother. He only had a moment to consider whose double dealing – as it must have appeared – was the worse, his or Sally's. But bringing her mother was really too bad. But now what was he to do about his own mother? The jury were about to be sworn. When was he to tell the judge? And in what language? How awful to have to get up and say, 'The lady's my mother,' like Strephon in *Iolanthe*. 'I suppose I'd better do it at once,' he said to himself, and very unhappily rose and looked at the judge, who simply shook his head at him and waved him to sit down. He did not feel he could speak to his next-door neighbour. It sounded too absurd. Being called by his Christian name at school was nothing. Oh, dear, this is a nice way to start. Will I ever recover? he thought. Now they were swearing the jury. He must do something. He got up again. The judge looked at him angrily. Even a layman should know that the swearing of the jury must not be interrupted. Applications could be made after they had been sworn. Here, was a member of the Bar not only getting up when he ought to have waited, but getting up again after he'd been told to sit down. He really must be taught a lesson.

'Yes, what is it?' he snapped to Roger. 'If you don't know the rules ask someone who does. I've told you to wait once.'

Roger remained standing, waiting to speak.

'Will you please sit down,' said the judge.

'My Lord, I want to mention – ' began Roger.

'I've told you to wait,' said the judge. All right, if the young man wanted it he should have it. He turned his body slightly towards counsel's seats.

'In this Court,' he said, 'where I have had the honour to preside for a good many years I have never yet seen counsel behave in this shocking manner. Justice could not be administered at all unless directions from the Bench were observed by the Bar. Until this moment, I have never known – '

Roger had had as much as he could stand and subsided, his face scarlet.

'Thank you,' said the judge. 'Thank you very much. I am very much obliged. Now perhaps the swearing of the jury can be continued.'

199

Although the jury could in this particular case have all been sworn at once, it is the practice at the Old Bailey to swear them separately. In due course it became Mrs Thursby's turn. It must be right to object. His client had been told that he must object when the jurors came to the Book to be sworn. Now was the time. He had a good mind to leave his mother on the jury. But then he supposed he'd be disbarred. Fearless integrity, the Treasurer of his Inn had said. That was all very well for him. He'd never had his mother on the jury. Well, he must do it, but there's nothing fearless about it, he said to himself. I'm terrified. He got up again. The judge could not have believed it possible. He was a choleric man, equally capable of bestowing immense and undeserved praise in fantastically flattering terms and of – figuratively – spitting like two cats. This time the cats had it.

'I do not know your name,' he began, thinking hard for the most offensive words he could find, 'but that,' he went on, 'in view of your extraordinary behaviour I do not find altogether surprising. Will you now do me the personal favour of resuming your seat. Otherwise I shall be under the painful duty of reporting you to your Benchers before whom it cannot have been very long ago that you appeared to be called to the Bar.'

As Roger still remained on his feet, waiting to speak, but not liking to interrupt the judge, from whom words poured steadily at him in a vitriolic stream, the judge said: 'I order you to sit down.'

Roger did as he was told and, from where he sat, said loudly and clearly – as though it were the last cry of a man about to be executed: 'I object to the next juror. She's my mother.'

There was an immediate and thrilling silence. It was broken by Mr Green.

'I don't, my Lord. In fact I like the look of the lady.'

'You be quiet,' said the judge, and thought for several seconds. During the time he had had the honour to preside in that Court he had seldom had to think for so long before making a decision. Eventually he tapped his desk with a pencil and asked the clerk for Roger's name. Then he spoke: 'Mr Thursby,' he began.

Roger did not know whether to get up or not. He'd been ordered to sit down. It would be contempt of Court to get up. Yet somehow when the judge was addressing him it seemed all wrong to remain seated. He did not know what to do until his next-door neighbour whispered.

'Get up. The old fool's going to apologize.'

Roger took the advice and was relieved to find that he was not immediately ordered to sit down – indeed if the judge had told two warders to throw him to the ground he would not have been altogether surprised.

'Mr Thursby,' repeated the judge in dulcet tones after Roger had risen, 'I owe you a very humble apology, and I hope you will see fit to accept it. I am extremely sorry. By my haste I have placed you in a position which would have been horribly embarrassing for any member of the Bar and which for one of – if I may say so without offence – your limited experience must have been almost beyond bearing. You dealt with the situation with a courage and a patience which I shall long remember.'

A lump came into Roger's throat, and it was all he could do to prevent himself from breaking down. He tried to say: 'Thank you, my Lord,' but very little was heard of it and he sat down and looked at his knees. The judge then turned to Mrs Thursby.

'You had better leave the jury box, madam. I owe you an apology too, and I should like to say that you have every reason for being proud of your son.'

To someone like Peter this would have been simply splendid. But it made Roger feel distinctly sick. And then he thought of all the people listening to him. Sally, Joy, Sally's mother and his own. Not to mention all the rest of those in Court. He felt as he had felt after boxing at school and being roundly trounced by a bigger boy, when the headmaster came up to him and said in a loud voice: 'Plucky boy.'

It sent shivers down his back. He wondered if this sort of thing happened to everyone. They couldn't often have barrister's mothers on the jury at all, let alone in cases where their sons were engaged. Another juryman was sworn. The judge scribbled a note which the usher brought to Roger. It said:

So very sorry. I shall be so pleased if you will bring your mother to see me during the adjournment. S K.

Roger did not know whether to answer it in writing or by bowing. He asked his neighbour.

'What do I do with this?'

'Just bow and grin.'

He did as he was told. The judge smiled back at him. The jury had now been sworn and were informed of the charge against the prisoner. They were told he had pleaded Not Guilty and that it was for them to say whether he was Guilty or not.

Counsel for the prosecution opened the case quite shortly and called as his first witness the man who had bought the toffee. His name was Blake. He was duly asked about his purchase from Mr Green and about the false reference.

'Would you have sent the money if you had not believed this document to be a genuine reference?'

'No.'

The moment arrived for Roger to cross-examine.

'You remember seeing the reference, I suppose?' he asked.

'Certainly.'

'Did you have any other letters about the same time?'

'Letters? Yes, of course.'

'From the defendant, I mean?'

'From the defendant? Only the one offering me the toffee.'

'How long was that before you received the reference?'

'Two or three weeks.'

'Quite sure?'

'Yes, I think so.'

That's what Henry meant, thought Roger. I shouldn't have asked that last question.

'Two to three weeks?' repeated Roger.

'Yes,' said Mr Blake.

This time Roger left it alone.

'Now, Mr Blake, you say you received the reference before you sent the money. Are you quite sure of that?'

'Certainly. Look at the date. The 20th. I sent the money on the 23rd. I must have received the reference on the 21st.'

'Got the envelope by any chance?'

'I don't keep envelopes.'

'So you're relying on your memory entirely?'

'Certainly not entirely. On the date on the reference as well.'

'So that if it hadn't had that date on it you wouldn't have known whether you sent the money before or after you received the reference?'

'I certainly would have. I sent it after I had the reference
– what's the point of being offered a reference if you don't
wait for it?'

'Does this in any way shake your recollection?' asked
Roger holding up the receipt for posting to be handed to
the witness. Mr Blake looked at it.

'Well?' he said.

'Does that shake your recollection at all?' asked Roger.

'Not in the least,' said the witness. 'It's just a receipt for
posting a letter.'

'To you.'

'What of it?'

'It was given to the prisoner.'

'How do I know?'

'What is this document?' asked the judge. 'Let me look
at it.' It was handed to the judge who looked at it closely.
'This is dated the 24th,' he said. 'It shows that a letter was
posted to you on that date by someone.'

'Yes, my Lord,' said the witness.

'Well,' said the judge, 'it apparently came into the
possession of the prisoner and if it was issued to him by
the post office it shows that he posted a letter to you on
the 24th.'

'Yes, my Lord?' said Mr Blake.

'Well – you've said that he only sent you one letter and
that was two or three weeks before you received the
reference.'

'Possibly I was wrong, my Lord.'

'Possibly anything,' said the judge, 'but what counsel
very properly puts to you is this. If that receipt was issued
to the prisoner are you still prepared to swear positively
that you received the reference before, you sent the
money?'

'I must have, my Lord.'

'Then how is this receipt to be accounted for?'

'I can't tell you that, my Lord, unless I had another letter from the prisoner. I suppose I might have.'

'But you can't remember one?'

'I can't say that I do, my Lord. Possibly, my Lord, the prisoner got it from someone else.'

'Whom do you suggest?'

'I have no idea, my Lord. All I know is that I was offered a reference and, if I'm offered a reference, I'm sure I wouldn't send the money without getting it first. I know something about this mail order business.'

'You mean you've been cheated before?' said Roger all too quickly.

'Steady,' said Mr Green.

'Be quiet and behave yourself,' said the judge. 'Your case is being conducted admirably. It is a model of what such a cross-examination should be. Perhaps, Mr Thursby,' he added, 'that last question could be rephrased.'

'Have you in the past been cheated?'

'I have.'

'Toffee?' asked Roger with a flash of inspiration.

'Yes, as a matter of fact,' said the witness.

'You've a sweet tooth?' asked Roger.

'Well, I have as a matter of fact.'

'You like toffee, apparently?'

'I don't see why I should be ashamed of it,' said Mr Blake.

'No one's suggesting you should be,' said the judge. 'Counsel only wishes to establish the fact that you are fond of toffee.'

'Well, I am,' said Mr Blake, 'and I don't mind admitting it.'

'P'raps you decided not to bother about a reference on this occasion and chanced sending the money?'

The witness did not answer.

'Well,' said the judge, 'what do you say to that?'

'I suppose it's possible,' said Mr Blake, 'but I don't think so.'

'It could have happened?' said the judge.

'I suppose so,' said Mr Blake reluctantly.

Eventually the case for the prosecution closed.

'Yes, Mr Thursby,' said the judge pleasantly. 'Are you going to open your case to the jury?'

What is this? thought Roger. He's inviting me to make two speeches. But I can't do that, surely. Henry said I couldn't, and I'm sure that's what it said in the book. But here he is inviting me to do so. It'll look rude if I don't accept his offer. He's being so nice to me. I mustn't offend him. P'raps it's a sort of consolation prize. Oh – well, here goes.

'If your Lordship pleases,' said Roger. 'May it please your Lordship, members of the jury, the evidence for the prosecution has been completed and it now becomes my duty to open the defence.'

How professional it sounded, thought Roger, as he said it. At that moment the judge suddenly realized that he might have misled Roger.

'Forgive me, Mr Thursby,' he said, 'but I assume that you are calling evidence in addition to the prisoner?'

'Oh, no, my Lord.'

'Well then,' said the judge, 'you can't have two speeches, you know. You address the jury afterwards.'

Well, I knew that, thought Roger. What's he want to make a ruddy fool of me for? Everybody will think I don't know a thing. Well, they're quite right but I don't want it advertised every moment. All right, here goes again.

'If your Lordship pleases. Mr Green, will you go into the witness box, please?'

'Certainly,' said Mr Green. 'With pleasure,' and he came out of the dock, and went into the box to be sworn. Roger asked him the necessary questions about himself and then asked: 'Who wrote the reference which was sent to Mr Blake?'

'I did.'

'When did you send it?'

'On the 24th February.'

'Do you identify the receipt for posting?'

'I do.'

'Did you write any other letter to Mr Blake except this reference and the original letter which he has produced?'

'I did not.'

'Did you obtain that receipt for posting from someone else or is it in respect of the reference?'

'It's in respect of the reference.'

'Thank you,' said Roger and sat down. Counsel for the prosecution then cross-examined.

'Let me follow this,' he said. 'Do I rightly understand your evidence to be this? You offered to supply toffee to Mr Blake, and offered to send him a reference. He does not wait for the reference but sends the money. After you have received the money you send him a reference which you have written out yourself in a false name. Is that your story?'

'That,' said Mr Green, 'is not only my story but it happens to be true. I hope you don't mind.'

'Don't be impertinent,' said the judge.

'I'm very sorry, my Lord,' said Mr Green. 'I don't intend to be impertinent but I have a little way of talking sometimes which makes people think that I do. Perhaps I'd better apologize in advance for any false impressions I may – '

'Be quiet,' said the judge, 'you're not doing yourself any good by making these silly speeches. Behave yourself and answer the questions.'

'Well, then,' said counsel, 'will you be good enough to tell my Lord and the jury why you thought it necessary after you'd received the money to send the reference?'

'For good measure,' said Mr Green. 'After all,' he went on, 'I'd offered a reference. Why shouldn't he have one? I thought it might make him happier.'

'Really,' said counsel, 'I completely fail to understand you.'

⸬'Ah,' said Mr Green, 'there are more things in heaven and earth, Horatio, than are dreamt of – '

'Now, look,' interrupted the judge, 'I shan't warn you again. If I have any more nonsense from you I shall stand this case over to next session.'

'I hope your Lordship won't do that,' said Mr Green. 'I may get another judge and I like being tried by your Lordship. There's nothing like a fair trial, I say.'

'Well, behave yourself,' said the judge, not altogether displeased.

'Makes you feel good, even if you aren't,' went on Mr Green. 'I'm so sorry, my Lord,' he added quickly.

'Mr Thursby,' said the judge, 'I must really ask you to control your client. I shan't warn him again.'

'If your Lordship pleases,' said Roger, not knowing how on earth he was to comply with the direction.

Fortunately Mr Green was a little less irrepressible for the rest of his evidence.

'Now,' said prosecuting counsel, 'is this the language you used about yourself in this admittedly false reference? "I have known Mr Arthur Green for many many years." '

'Quite true,' said Mr Green. 'I had.'

'Wait,' said counsel. 'Does it go on like this? "And during that period I can say that I have given him credit for thousands of pounds." Was that true?'

'Well, I've trusted him all my life,' said Mr Green, 'and he's never let me down.'

'Has he ever been worth thousands of pounds?'

'He's worth more than that to me,' said Mr Green.

'Did the reference go on like this?' asked counsel.

' "In my view he is in a very substantial way of business and can be trusted for any amount. Knowing him as I do I cannot well say less." Were you in a very substantial way of business?'

'Well, it's a comparative term. I was getting a lot of orders.'

'By sending false references?'

'Oh, dear, no – I always sent the references afterwards. I told you already.'

'I cannot see the object.'

'I'm sorry,' said Mr Green. 'I've done my best to explain and got into trouble with his Lordship in trying to do so.'

'Do you say this was an honest transaction?'

'Certainly. I got the money and he got the toffee.'

'Not all he ordered.'

'There's nothing about that in the indictment,' said Mr Green.

'Never mind about the indictment,' said counsel.

'But I do. That's what I'm being tried on, isn't it? It says I obtained goods by giving a false reference. Well, I didn't. Isn't that the end of the case?'

'Don't ask me questions,' said counsel, 'and kindly answer mine. Did not Mr Blake get less toffee than he paid for?'

'That's possible,' said Mr Green. 'I had a very bad man doing the packing at that time. He made away with a lot of toffee. Must have had a sweet tooth too. So it's quite possible Mr Blake got too little. But that wasn't my fault. I can't stand over the man who's doing the packing all the time, can I? I've got other work to do. And I'd no reason to distrust him at the time.'

'Who was this man?'

'Well, the name he gave to me was Brown – without an "e" – but, of course, it might have been an alias.'

'Did you get a reference with him?'

'I don't much care for references,' said Mr Green. 'You see – ' he added and waved his hand expressively.

'Are you sure there ever was a Mr Brown?'

'Of course,' said Mr Green. 'I can describe him if you like. Aged about thirty-five, middling height, brown hair, turned his toes in as he walked, small moustache – though, of course, he might have shaved it off now. Fond of toffee,' he added.

Prosecuting counsel paused.

'Yes, Mr Thackeray?' said the judge. 'Any more questions?'

'I suggest,' said counsel, 'that you sent the reference before you received the money.'

For answer Mr Green just waved the receipt.

'Will you answer my question?' asked counsel angrily.

'Well, Mr Thackeray,' said the judge, 'it is a pretty good answer, isn't it? Can you really do much more with this case? After all, it is for you to prove your case with reasonable certainty. No one likes false references – I don't suppose the jury do any more than you – but you've got to prove it was received before your client sent the money.'

'There is the evidence of Mr Blake,' said counsel.

'I know,' said the judge, 'but how far can that take you in a criminal trial? He was by no means certain about it – and here is the receipt. That is a genuine document, anyway. What the truth of this transaction is, I don't pretend to know, but the prisoner's quite right when he says he's being tried on this indictment which simply alleges one false pretence. I can't, of course, say there's no evidence – but it may be that the jury will say they have heard enough already.'

'My Lord, the question of attempting to obtain by false pretences could arise.'

'Surely not,' said the judge. 'How can he attempt to obtain money which he has already received?'

The judge turned towards the jury.

'Members of the jury,' he said, 'once the case for the prosecution is closed it is open for you at any stage to say you've heard enough and that you're not satisfied that the prisoner's guilt has been proved. You may think his methods of carrying on business are pretty odd – you may think that a little more investigation might have been made by the police into those methods – and such investigations can still be made. But there is only one charge against the prisoner and that has to be proved to your satisfaction. Perhaps you'd like to have a word with each other.'

The jury did as they were told and three minutes later they stopped the case and returned a verdict of Not Guilty.

'Thank you,' said Mr Green when the judge discharged him. 'May I say something, my Lord?' he asked.

'Well, what is it?' asked the judge.

'I should like to thank you for a very fair trial, my Lord.' The judge said nothing, but he did not in the least object. 'Would I be out of order,' went on Mr Green, 'in inviting everyone to some mild form of celebration?'

'Be quiet,' snapped the judge. 'I've a good mind to send you to prison for contempt of Court.'

'Oh, that's different,' said Mr Green. 'I'd better go.' And he left the dock. He went straight to Roger, shook hands with him and whispered: 'What did I tell you? Can you sing now?'

Roger said nothing.

'Would you like my card?' said Mr Green. 'In case I can be of any help to you in the future?'

'Goodbye,' said Roger.

'Goodbye,' said Mr Green, and started to go. Then he came back.

'Oh, if at any time you should want any toffee – ' he said, and went again.

CHAPTER TWENTY-ONE

A Jewel of a Husband

The judge rose for lunch immediately afterwards and Roger, as he had been bidden, took his mother to see him in his room.

'What do I call him?' she asked. 'I've never met a judge before. I don't want to do the wrong thing. I'd hate to disgrace you.'

'You call him "Sir Stuart," said Roger. 'I call him "Judge," I think.'

They went to the judge's room.

'I would like to congratulate you again,' he said to Roger's mother, 'on the very brilliant beginning your son has made. He will go a very long way and you should be very proud of him.'

'Thank you very much,' she said. 'I'm so glad he was able to be of some use.'

'Mother's never been to the Old Bailey before,' said Roger quickly.

'No,' said Mrs Thursby. 'I found it most interesting, and the flowers and herbs and things give it such a friendly, cosy air. Even the prisoner can't mind too much in such a charming atmosphere. It's more like a garden party really.'

'I'm not sure,' said the judge, 'that our invitations are always as welcome.'

'As a matter of fact,' said Mrs Thursby. 'I nearly mislaid mine and it was only by chance that I got here at all. Would you have been very angry if I hadn't come?'

'I'm afraid my mother doesn't quite appreciate the seriousness of a jury summons, Judge,' said Roger hurriedly. 'I'll make sure she knows next time. If I'd known this time, it wouldn't have happened. It was a dreadful shock for me when I saw her in the jury box.'

'Well, all's well that ends well,' said the judge. 'Is this your first visit to the Old Bailey?' he added.

'I've been coming here with Grimes for several days. I'm his pupil, Judge,' said Roger.

'Indeed?' said the judge. 'A remarkably fine piece of cross-examination for a pupil. Quite the best I've heard.'

'Thank you very much indeed,' said Roger, 'and thank you, too, for being so nice to me.'

'I'm not sure about that,' said the judge, 'but I'll try to make up for what happened earlier if you'll come and see me at the end of the day. I'll send these flowers to your mother.' He indicated the bouquet which went into Court with him. 'That is, if she'd do me the honour of accepting them.'

'Oh, Sir Stuart, that is most kind,' said Mrs Thursby. 'I shall be thrilled. I've never had flowers from a judge before. Oh, yes, I did once now I come to think of it. My husband knew one of the judges who gave licences and things to public houses. He sent me some carnations. I suppose you do that too.'

'Licensing justices,' said the judge, not entirely pleased at the comparison. 'No, that is rather different. Well, I'm very glad to have met you and once again I congratulate you upon your son,' and he got up to indicate that the interview was at an end.

None too soon, thought Roger. I wonder what else mother might have said. He took her out to lunch, then she went home and he returned to Court.

The first case he heard after lunch was a plea of Guilty by a woman who had run away from her husband and married someone else. She was charged with bigamy and obtaining credit by fraud from a boarding house where they'd spent their bigamous honeymoon. The judge sent the man to prison and then proceeded to deal with the woman. He was informed that her husband was prepared to take her back again.

'You're a very wicked woman,' he said to the weeping prisoner. 'You have a jewel of a husband – ' he stopped in the middle. 'Let him come forward,' he added.

A moment later the prisoner's husband went into the witness box.

'A jewel of a husband,' repeated the judge. 'Now, Mr Grant,' he said, looking in the most friendly manner at the husband, 'I understand you're prepared to take your wife back in spite of everything. Magnificent. That is so, isn't it?'

'My heart's full,' said the man.

'Quite so,' said the judge. 'He very properly says that his heart is full. Most proper. A jewel of a husband. But you are prepared to take her back?'

'My heart's full,' repeated the husband.

'Quite so,' said the judge still beaming at him. 'We all understand that. Very natural. But you are prepared to take her back?'

The man did not answer for a moment.

The judge's brow started to cloud ever so slightly.

'You are prepared to take her back?' he repeated.

'My heart's – ' began the man.

'Yes, yes, I know. Very proper. But you are prepared to take her back?'

'Full,' said the man.

'Mr Grant,' said the judge in less kindly tones. 'Would you be good enough to answer my question?'

'Very difficult, my Lord,' said the man. 'My heart's full.'

'Look here,' said the judge, his patience rapidly becoming exhausted, 'are you prepared to take her back or not?'

'If you say so, my Lord,' said the man.

'It's not for me to say one way or the other. She's your wife and it's for you to make up your mind. If you don't take her back I shall probably send her to prison.'

'How long for?' said the man.

'Don't ask me questions,' said the judge.

The man remained silent.

'Well, which is it to be?' said the judge. 'We can't wait all night for you.'

Still no answer.

'Well?' the judge almost shouted.

Roger reflected that the case had now progressed some way from the 'jewel of a husband' stage.

'I don't think six months would do her any harm,' said the man, 'and it would give me time to think.'

'Now look,' said the judge, 'when you married this woman you took her for better or worse.'

'It seems to have been worse,' said the man.

'Will you be quiet while I'm speaking,' said the judge angrily. 'Have you never heard of charity?'

'Charity,' said the man, 'begins at home. She left home.'

'I'm not going to argue with you,' said the judge. 'If you lack all decent feeling, I can't give it to you, but, if you don't forgive her, it may be on your conscience for the rest of your life.'

216

'What about her conscience?' said the man. 'How would you like your wife to go running off with the lodger?'

'Take that man away,' said the judge, and the husband left the witness box.

'Now, Margaret Grant, I'm not going to send you to prison. Dry your eyes and listen. You've behaved very stupidly – yes – and wickedly, but the exact circumstances of your married life are known only to you, and the man who was just standing in the witness box.'

The woman opened her mouth as though to speak.

'Yes, what is it?' asked the judge. 'You want to say something?'

'Only this, my Lord,' faltered the woman.

'Yes?' said the judge in a kind, encouraging tone.

'He's a jewel of a husband, my Lord.'

I'm glad I stayed, thought Roger.

CHAPTER TWENTY-TWO

Offer of a Brief

Roger left the Old Bailey feeling happier than at any time since he was called to the Bar. He had defended his first prisoner and he had got him off. The judge had praised him and congratulated him on his cross-examination. It was almost unbelievable. Mr Green no doubt had friends and perhaps he would send them to him. He could almost hear people saying already: 'He must have a chance, Thursby's defending him.'

He went back to chambers very elated, and at once went to Henry.

'Well, how did you get on?'

'I got him off.'

'Well done you. Jolly good. Tell me all about it.'

Roger told him everything.

'One thing perhaps,' said Henry, 'I ought to warn you about.'

'Oh?'

'Compliments from the Bench. You'll get them, you know, and you'll feel hugely pleased and think you've made your name and all that. For example, if you go to the Old Bailey again you will hear the old boy say: "Members of the jury, you have just heard what in my opinion is a model of a speech from counsel for the prisoner. Since I have had the honour to preside at this Court – " and so on and so forth. I'm sorry to have to tell you, old boy,' went on Henry, 'that it don't mean a thing. Indeed, when that stops happening from that particular quarter it means that you really have made a little headway.'

'Oh,' said Roger, a little disappointed. 'Then wasn't my cross-examination any good then?'

'I didn't hear it, but from what you tell me I should say it was very good. All I'm warning you about is not to be too elated when a judge plasters you with good things. There *are* compliments from the Bench which are greatly to be valued. But they are rare – and at your present stage you don't know which is which. You don't mind my telling you all this?'

'Of course not.'

'I'm only doing it because no one told me. And it was the most frightful disappointment to me after His Honour Judge Smoothe had lauded me to the skies – and incidentally decided against me – to find that clients weren't queuing up to brief me. Later on, if you look around any Court presided over by a judge who indulges in fulsome praise of counsel, you'll see looks being exchanged between experienced counsel and solicitors. The best judges and those whose praise is worth having don't do it. But cheer up. You got him off and that's the chief thing. Now I suppose you're going to celebrate with Sally. Or could I hope that it's Joy?'

'Quite frankly, I hadn't thought,' said Roger. 'Oh – hell,' he added. 'I'm in for a spot of trouble there. But I won't worry you with it.'

'Look,' said Henry, 'perhaps I shouldn't ask this, but would you very much mind if I did ask Sally to come out some time? I'll understand perfectly if you object.'

'Of course not,' said Roger. 'I think it jolly decent of you to want to.'

'I'm not sure that that's what I'd call it,' said Henry, 'but I'll try to behave.'

When Roger got home that evening he at once telephoned Sally. What had she thought of him? He was dying to know.

'Hello, Sally,' he said.

'Hello, Roger,' she said somewhat coldly.

He couldn't help that. He must know what she thought.

'Sally, what did you think? I'm longing to know. Was I any better?'

'As a liar, d'you mean?' said Sally. 'Yes, I think you've made quite remarkable progress in a very short time.'

'Oh, Sally – you must let me explain. You mean about Joy being there?'

'And you're so quick too.'

'Sally – you must let me explain. I'd no idea when I spoke to you that Joy was coming. Really I hadn't.'

'She just happened to come, I suppose? What with your mother being on the jury, the day was pretty full of coincidences for you.'

'Oh, Sally, please listen. I had to take her.'

'Oh, it wasn't a coincidence? You just changed your mind about taking her, was that it? Well, I suppose everyone's entitled to change his mind.'

'Which reminds me,' said Roger. 'What were you doing there? It was you who advised me not to have anyone there. And you not only come but you bring your mother too. The whole blooming outfit.'

'Don't you call my mother an outfit,' said Sally.

'Look,' said Roger, 'can't we meet and get things straight?'

So they met and everything was explained as far as it could be.

'It looks as though Joy's uncle is going to be pretty useful to you,' said Sally.

'It does, doesn't it?' said Roger brightly.

'And what other Herculean tasks d'you imagine he'll impose on you in return. Marrying Joy, d'you think?'

'Oh, don't, Sally. It isn't fair. I wouldn't be human if I didn't want to get on.'

'There are ways and ways of getting on. If you're in love with Joy, all right, splendid. Another excellent coincidence. Go ahead, marry her and let her uncle keep you.'

'You're being beastly.'

'Plain, if you like,' said Sally. 'If, on the other hand, you're not in love with Joy – well – what was the word you used – beastly, wasn't it? Oh, Roger dear, can't you get on without making up to Joy in order to get work out of her uncle?'

'It sounds awful putting it that way.'

'Well, how would you put it – if you're not in love with her? And if you go on doing it long enough you'll find you have to marry the girl.'

'I'm much too young to marry, anyway,' said Roger, 'and I haven't any money.'

'That's what I mean. If Joy's uncle provides the income – you can't very decently marry someone else on it – when you do marry.'

'I can't very well refuse the briefs.'

'If you stop taking Joy out, they'll stop too.'

Roger thought for a moment.

'You are right, Sally,' he said. 'At least I suppose so. You'd say it was rather like those men who – well, you know what I mean.'

'Oh, I wouldn't put it quite like that,' said Sally. 'But it does seem a bit mean.'

'All right,' said Roger, 'I'll stop. I'll tell Joy straight out that I'll never marry her. Then if her uncle still keeps on sending me briefs, that's his affair, isn't it? After all, the time may come when he briefs me for my own sake.'

'We'll drink to that,' said Sally.

And they did.

'Roger,' said his mother that evening.

'Yes, darling?'

'How long d'you think it'll be before you're earning real money? I mean, flowers are all very nice, but they don't pay the bills.'

'Oh, Mother – I'm afraid it may be an awful long time. I hope not, but it is a slow job, I'm afraid, unless one's awfully lucky.'

'What d'you mean by slow?' said Mrs Thursby. 'You wouldn't be likely to have two hundred pounds to spare next Thursday?'

'Mother – what do you mean?'

'Oh, well – never mind,' said Mrs Thursby. 'It doesn't matter.'

'Why, Mother darling, what is it?'

'I did rather a stupid thing, I'm afraid. I lent Elsie some money – to pay her bootmakers I thought she said. It seemed an awful lot for shoes, but still she's always so well turned out I thought she couldn't have paid them for some years. But it was her Scots accent. It was really her bookmakers. And now she's lost some more and can't pay me back when she promised. Oh, well – it only means the gas and telephone may be a bit cut off.'

'The telephone!' said Roger in horror.

'Well, we didn't always have them.'

'But I might have something frightfully urgent. Alec might want to get hold of me.'

'Oh, well, never mind. P'raps they'll forget to cut ours off. They must have a lot of others to deal with. Then if they do, we can always get an electric cooker. I've sometimes wondered whether I wouldn't prefer one.'

'But the telephone, Mother. We must find the money for that. How much do you owe altogether?'

'I never had much head for figures, but if Elsie had sent that two hundred pounds back it would be quite all right.'

'You didn't lend her two hundred pounds, Mother?'

'Well, she seemed to want it so badly. And I'd just had my quarterly cheque. It was to come back in a month. And d'you know she said she'd add another fifty pounds. That was very nice of her, I thought. I'm sure she meant to. I'd trust her anywhere, if you know what I mean.'

'Backing horses is just lunacy,' said Roger.

'Not according to Elsie. She said it was only a temporary setback. She said she made a large profit every year.'

'So does everyone,' said Roger. 'That's why bookmakers smoke fat cigars. Oh, well – I suppose we'll manage somehow or other. But it is a bit of a blow.'

The telephone rang.

'Hullo, oh, hullo, Joy – yes – what – can't you say it on the telephone? It can't be as secret as all that. Oh, all right. I'll be along.' He turned to his mother.

'Joy's got something she must tell me. I suppose I shall have to go. Shan't be long.'

Roger decided to take advantage of the occasion and break the news to Joy as he'd agreed with Sally. Just as well to get it over. He went straight to her rooms. She was waiting on the doorstep.

'Oh, Roger, I thought you were never coming. Oh, Roger darling, I thought you were wonderful, getting that funny little man off and the judge apologizing to you and everything.'

'It wasn't too bad,' said Roger modestly. 'But one mustn't let things like that go to one's head. Henry said it didn't really mean a thing.'

'Well,' said Joy, 'see if this means a thing.'

'What is it?'

'It's so terrific you won't believe it. Oh, I am a lucky girl. You know the big sausage people – Baggallys?'

'Yes, of course.'

'Well, apparently somebody's been copying their sausages or something and they're bringing a huge action. I believe it's called a patent action.' She pronounced it like patent in patent shoes.

'Patent,' corrected Roger. He wouldn't have known it had a short 'a' if Henry hadn't told him.

'Well?' said Roger puzzled.

'Well, Uncle Alfred is their solicitor, and he's going to send a brief in it to you.'

'Me?' said Roger. 'But it's ridiculous. I don't know anything about patents. Even if I did I couldn't do a case of that size.'

'You won't be all by yourself,' said Joy. 'There are three other counsel in it besides you. There's, let me see, Sir George Pratt – Uncle Alfred says he's the chief man on the subject – and then there are two others and then there's you. So you'll get some help, you see. Oh, and Uncle Alfred's coming round to explain it to you himself. That's why you had to come at once. He'll be here in a moment.'

No doubt Roger ought to have acted at once on what might be called the Sally plan. But he could hardly be blamed for just waiting to see what Uncle Alfred said first. Anyway, there wasn't enough time to say to Joy what he had intended to say. He'd have to wrap it up a bit. And that takes time. And then Uncle Alfred arrived.

'My dear Roger, you must forgive this informality – but I hope that, now that I might say you're almost one of the family you will forgive me. Now, my dear boy,' he went on without giving Roger a chance to interrupt, 'I want your help, your personal help. And I want to have a word with you before taking official action. I don't know whether Joy has told you that we've quite an important action for Baggallys. Now – I don't want you to think I'm not satisfied with the counsel we've so far briefed in the case. I am indeed. But I can't help feeling that in a case of this kind an outside view from one of the younger generation would be a help. We've all eaten sausages for so long that we may have got into a rut with our ideas. So, to cut a long story short, I want you – as a personal favour to me – to accept a junior brief in the matter. I must apologize for not mentioning it to you at an earlier stage, but, to be quite candid, it was Mr Smith's idea and he only had it quite recently.'

'Well, it's most awfully kind of you, Mr Merivale.'

'And there is one other matter. And I hope you'll forgive my mentioning that to you personally too. I know that counsel and solicitors don't discuss fees together. As far as you and I are concerned it's done for nothing. It's the clerk, who deals with the fees. But this is rather an embarrassing situation and that's why I'd be grateful for your help. You see, my firm's an old-fashioned one. We haven't moved forward like some of the others. Now, of course you're aware, my dear boy, of the two-thirds rule. Well, my firm have always stuck to that, even when the Bar Council agreed with the Law Society that we needn't. So that, for example, Sir George has got three thousand guineas on his brief, Wincaster two thousand and Soames one thousand three hundred and thirty-three. Now quite frankly, my dear boy, we can't run to more than, say, four hundred for your brief. Not that you wouldn't be worth more, but we couldn't run to it. Now when Mr Smith approaches your clerk on the matter, your clerk who's used to our old-fashioned ways will expect two-thirds of one thousand three hundred and thirty-three, and it would be most embarrassing for Mr Smith. So what I want to know, my dear boy, is whether you will very kindly have a word with your clerk in advance and ask him to accept four hundred on the brief – that's, of course, if you're willing yourself – and only if you're willing – I realize that it's rather a lot to ask, but I thought as a personal favour to me you might possibly be prepared to consider it. Of course, there'll be refreshers – about a hundred a day I should think – and I suppose the case ought to last about six weeks. So your total fees in the matter ought to be between three and four thousand pounds. That's, of course, in the Court below. It's bound to go to the Court of Appeal and probably to the House of Lords. Now, my boy, will you do it? I'm not pressing you at all – but it would be a kindness.'

Roger looked out of the window.

'It's terribly good of you,' he said. 'May I think it over?'

'I beg your pardon?' said Mr Merivale. 'My hearing isn't quite as good as it was. I didn't quite catch what you said.'

'May I think it over?' repeated Roger.

Mr Merivale put his hand through his hair several times. 'I only do this, young man,' he said, 'when I am surprised to the point of being astounded.'

'I want to ask advice,' said Roger.

'Advice?' said Mr Merivale. 'Advice is it? Well, my advice to you, young man, is that you should consult the nearest brain specialist. And another piece of advice is this: if you don't seize all the opportunities you're given at the Bar you won't get very far. I don't believe that there is any young man at the Bar who would have said what you did. Admittedly you have a very fine practice. But there must be days when you don't receive a brief marked four hundred guineas. Of course, the one thousand guinea briefs help to make up for it, but if what I'm told is true, there aren't as many of those as there used to be. And dock briefs – or should I say one dock brief at the Old Bailey – hardly seems to take their place. But no doubt you know best. May I take it then that you're too busy to accept the instructions? Or is it that you would consider it undignified to accept less than two-thirds of Mr Soames' fee?'

Roger looked out of the window again and then blood suddenly rushed to his head. He had had the experience before and he had it again several times later in his career. When blood rushes like that to a man's head he may win a VC, commit suicide, marry the girl or say something he will regret or be proud of for the rest of his life. Roger did not know whether he would be proud or sorry, but he knew he must say it. When blood rushes like that to the head there is indeed no option. The thing has to be done or said. There is one course and one course only which has to be taken, whatever the cost. Through the window Roger could see a prostitute leaning against some railings.

'Yes, Mr Merivale,' he said. 'Undignified. That's the word.'

CHAPTER TWENTY-THREE

Henry's Case

Three months later Henry was dining with Sally.

'You're the nicest man I know,' she said.

'You know what I think of you,' he said, 'and that by itself shows I'm not. I knew what would happen if I took you out to dinner. When you first briefed me in order to be near Roger I knew that, unless I took a very firm hold of myself, I should fall in love with you. So far from taking hold of myself I asked Roger if he'd mind. And here we are.'

'Yes,' said Sally, 'here we are. And there's nothing to be done about it.'

'P'raps it's as well,' said Henry. 'I shouldn't think very much of myself if you cared for me. As it is, it's all right. The only person who's in trouble is me. I must admit I rather like it.'

'I'm in trouble too,' said Sally.

'Ah, but you were before I met you. So I've no responsibility for that.'

'How is he doing? You think he'll get on, don't you?'

'I'm quite sure he will. He works like a black and he never believes anything anyone says to him until he's seen it's right. He's a certainty. How long it'll take before he really gets going, I don't know. But once it starts it'll come with a rush. And you'll see he'll develop. He's got all the right instincts. A certain degree of priggishness may be an advantage to begin with at the Bar.'

'Tell me another thing – you needn't if you don't want to. Have I a chance?'

'You tell me and I'll tell you,' said Henry.

'Don't be flippant, please.'

'I was not being flippant, I assure you. It's much worse at thirty-three than it is at twenty-one. I know. I've had both. You only know what it's like at twenty-one.'

'It's terrible, Henry. Do please tell me. I'd believe almost anything you tell me. But I shan't believe you if you say "no." Since he gave up Joy I thought something might have happened. But it hasn't.'

'Poor Joy,' said Henry. 'She overdid it.'

'That isn't an answer, Henry. Or is it intended to be the kindest way? You are kind, Henry. I'd trust you anywhere. Who'd think of asking an interested party like you?'

'It is a compliment, I agree. No, I've often tried to think what's the answer to your question. And the only one I can give is "yes". '

'D'you mean it, Henry?'

'Of course I do. But you mustn't be too optimistic; he's much too wrapped up in his work. He thinks of very little else. He hasn't had a brief since he broke with Joy, but he might have a large practice if one judged from the amount of work he does. He's still terribly young, but he's developing. And, of course, he'll fall in love. And it could be with you. He'll be a blithering idiot, if he doesn't.'

'Dear Henry – how lovely to be with you. You're the nicest man I know.'

'No chance of promotion?' said Henry.

Sally shook her head. 'I doubt it,' she said.

'Oh, well,' said Henry. 'No case is ever lost till judgment is given, and even then there can be an appeal.'

CHAPTER TWENTY-FOUR

The Stigma

Roger's year was nearly at an end when one day Alec came into the pupils' room. Peter had left by this time and there were two new pupils. Roger was now the senior.

'I've got you a brief, sir,' said Alec.

'Oh, Alec, how splendid,' said Roger. 'What is it?'

'It's only a judgment summons,' said Alec, 'but you never know what it may lead to.'

'Thank you very much,' said Roger and seized the papers eagerly. He found that he was in the comparatively unusual position of being briefed for the judgment debtor. Usually it is only the judgment creditor who is represented. For fairly obvious reasons. The debtor has no money to spare on engaging solicitors, let alone counsel. As always, Roger had a chat with Henry about it and in consequence he took Henry's advice and went to the County Court where the case was to be heard in order to see how the judge there, Judge Perkins, treated judgment summonses.

'They vary so tremendously,' Henry had said. 'Some judges don't seem to require any evidence of means worth speaking of and make committal orders right and left. Others hardly ever make them. I must say I think the whole thing's a bit out of date.'

At one County Court which Roger had visited the dialogue during the hearing of judgment summonses had usually been like this:

CLERK: 'British Loan Company against Brown.'

SOLICITOR: 'I appear for the judgment creditor, your Honour.'

JUDGE: 'Well, Mr Brown, have you any offer to make?'

BROWN: 'I'm very sorry I've got into arrears, your Honour, but – '

JUDGE: 'Never mind about that for the moment. Have you any offer to make?'

BROWN: 'Well, it's so difficult, your Honour, with the wife ill and being out of work myself – '

JUDGE: 'I'll go into all of that if necessary, but tell me first if you have any offer of any kind to make. This debt has got to be paid, you know.'

BROWN: 'I might manage ten shillings a week, your Honour.'

JUDGE: 'What do you say, Mr Worcester?'

SOLICITOR: 'I'll take that with a committal order, your Honour.'

JUDGE: 'Very well, then. Committal order for fourteen days, suspended so long as two pounds a month is paid. Now, do you know what that means, Mr Brown?'

BROWN: 'I have to pay two pounds a month.'

JUDGE: 'It means rather more than that, Mr Brown. It means that as long as you do pay two pounds a month all will be well – but, if you don't, then the bailiff will come and arrest you and take you to prison for fourteen days.'

BROWN: 'But suppose I can't pay, your Honour?'

JUDGE: 'I've told you what will happen if you don't pay. You should have thought of that before you borrowed the money. Call the next case, please.'

But Judge Perkins dealt with them differently. The first which Roger heard him dispose of was:

CLERK: 'James Brothers against Smith.'

SOLICITOR: 'I appear for the judgment creditor, your Honour.'

JUDGE: 'Any offer to make, Mr Smith?'

SMITH: 'A pound a month, your Honour.'

JUDGE: 'What do you say, Mr Bray?'

SOLICITOR: 'If your Honour will reinforce it with a committal order – '

JUDGE: 'You know perfectly well, Mr Bray, that I can't do that without evidence of means.'

SOLICITOR: 'But he's offered a pound a month, your Honour.'

JUDGE: 'That is simply a promise for the future. To my mind it is no evidence whatever that he has the money now or has had it in the past. Question him about his means if you wish.'

The solicitor questioned Mr Smith about his means but without much effect, and eventually the judge simply made an order for him to pay one pound per month, with no penalty attached for non-payment.

The dialogue in the next one was as follows:

SOLICITOR: 'Now Mr Davies, what do you earn?'

DAVIES: 'It varies.'

SOLICITOR: 'What does it average?'

DAVIES: 'Oh – seven to eight pounds.'

SOLICITOR: 'What about overtime?'

DAVIES: 'I don't do a lot.'

SOLICITOR: 'How much on an average?'

DAVIES: 'I don't know.'

SOLICITOR: 'You must have some idea. If necessary, you know, your firm can be brought here to prove what you do earn.'

DAVIES: 'Last week I didn't do any overtime at all.'

SOLICITOR: 'What about the week before?'

DAVIES: 'I forget.'

JUDGE: 'Mr Davies, you must try to remember. You must know roughly what you average for overtime each week.'

DAVIES: 'Some weeks I don't do any.'

JUDGE: 'Mr Davies, if you persist in avoiding an answer to the question, I shall assume that you earn seven to eight pounds a week overtime.'

DAVIES: 'It's nothing like as much as that.'

JUDGE: 'How much is it, then?'

DAVIES: 'Not more than two to three pounds.'

JUDGE: 'Very well then. Your average earnings are about ten pounds a week.'

SOLICITOR: 'Possibly more?'

DAVIES: 'Not more.'

SOLICITOR: 'Whom d'you have to keep out of your ten pounds?'

DAVIES: 'My wife.'

SOLICITOR: 'Does she do any work?'

DAVIES: 'She does a bit.'

SOLICITOR: 'How much does she earn?'

DAVIES: 'I've no idea.'

SOLICITOR: 'You must have some idea.'

DAVIES: 'We don't discuss it. It's her business.'

JUDGE: 'No doubt it is, but I should have thought you might have taken sufficient interest in her affairs to know about how much she earned.' (*Pause.*) 'Well, don't you?'

DAVIES: 'She gets a few pounds, I dare say.'

SOLICITOR: 'What is your rent?'

DAVIES: 'Has this anything to do with the case?'

JUDGE: 'It certainly has.'

DAVIES: 'I don't pay rent. I'm buying the house through a building society – at least the wife is. I just guarantee the payments.'

SOLICITOR: 'How much are they?'

DAVIES: 'Eight pounds three shillings and four pence a month.'

SOLICITOR: 'Have you any other debts?'

DAVIES: 'That's my affair.'

JUDGE: 'You will answer the question. Have you any other debts?'

DAVIES: 'Not that I know of.'

SOLICITOR: 'Why haven't you paid anything off this judgment?'

DAVIES: 'Because it isn't justice. He hit me first.'

JUDGE: 'That matter has already been decided. There is a judgment against you. How much a month do you offer?'

DAVIES: 'Five shillings.'

JUDGE: 'You're just trifling with the Court. Is there anything else you want to say before I make an order?'

DAVIES: 'It doesn't seem much use.'

JUDGE: 'Mr Davies, you will be detained until the rising of the Court and I shall then consider whether to fine you or send you to prison for contempt of Court. Meanwhile, I shall deal with this summons. You will be committed to prison for six weeks and the order will be suspended so long as you pay five pounds per month.'

DAVIES: 'I can't do it.'

JUDGE: 'Then you know the alternative. I am quite satisfied that you could have paid off the whole of this debt by now and have deliberately refrained from doing so.'

In the next case, before Judge Perkins the debtor admitted that he went in for football pools in a small way. The judge immediately made a committal order.

'You can't gamble with your creditor's money,' he said. 'It's not my concern whether you bet or not in the ordinary way, but if you could send half a crown a week to the pool promoters you could have sent it to the plaintiff, and you ought to have done so. Committal order for twenty-one days suspended so long as one pound per month is paid.'

The next case was an even worse one. The debt was due to a wine merchant and the debtor admitted that he had been going to greyhound racing regularly ever since.

'This is quite outrageous,' said the judge. 'You will be committed to prison for six weeks and I shall suspend the order for seven days only. If the whole amount is not paid within that time, the order for your imprisonment will be effective.'

'But I can't pay twenty-five pounds in seven days,' said the alarmed debtor.

'Then you will spend six weeks in prison,' said the judge. 'I have no sympathy whatever with you. You buy drink on credit, don't pay for it and spend the money you could have used to pay for it on going to the races.'

Roger went back to chambers feeling that he knew Judge Perkins' methods of dealing with judgment summonses fairly well. A day or two later he had a conference with his client, a cheerful gentleman called Starling. He came with his wife, who was also cheerful and was, in addition, an attractive young woman. They were brought by their solicitor, Mr Fergus Trent, who was an old friend of theirs.

'Well, here we are,' said Mr Starling. 'When's the party?'

'Next Tuesday.'

'That's awkward. 'Fraid we shan't be able to come. It's Lingfield that day.'

'D'you mean the races?' said Roger, a little alarmed.

'Don't be so prim and proper,' said Mrs Starling. 'Don't tell me you've never had a little flutter.'

'Well, just on the Derby, you know. I've never been to a race meeting, as a matter of fact, only to point-to-points.'

'Well, you ought to, old boy,' said Mr Starling. 'Do you a power of good. Champagne and brandy to begin with. Take a lovely girl with you. And you'll be on top of the world. I just take my wife. She's still pretty high in the handicap.'

'I say, you know,' said Roger, 'this is rather serious. I don't know if you realize it.'

'Serious, old boy? I'll say it is.'

'I'm glad you appreciate that,' said Roger.

'I meant if we couldn't go to Lingfield,' said Mr Starling. 'We always do well there.'

'Look,' said Roger, 'this judge sends people to prison.'

Mrs Starling laughed.

'Don't try and frighten us,' she said, 'that stopped a long time ago.'

'But he does really. What was this debt for?'

'Repairs to a car, old boy. Had a nasty smash in the Watford by-pass. Between you and me I was a bit pickled. But I got through the tests all right. And Sheila was a brick. Said she'd been with me all the evening – when she knew in fact that I'd been out with some of the boys. I told you she was class, didn't I? Real thoroughbred. Never have to ride her in blinkers.'

'The other way round sometimes, darling,' said his wife.

'I'm afraid I don't follow all this,' said Roger, 'but you're going to be in great difficulty before this particular judge. Let me see. The debt's forty pounds. Judgment was obtained three months ago. Now can you honestly swear you've lost nothing on horses since then?'

'Come again,' said Mr Starling.

Roger repeated the question.

'Old boy,' said Mr Starling, 'I can honestly swear, cross my heart and all that – I can honestly swear that we haven't *won* a penny. Otherwise, we'd have paid.'

'How much have you lost?'

'Is that fair, old boy? Don't rub it in. Why, Sheila actually sold a couple of dresses. Talk of taking the clothes off your back.'

'Mr Starling,' said Roger, 'I'm afraid this is going to be rather a shock for you. I know this judge, Judge Perkins, and unless you can pay the whole of that forty pounds within a week from Tuesday next, he'll send you to prison for six weeks.'

'You're not serious, old boy?'

'I am, absolutely.'

'But that's terrible. I couldn't possibly go to jail. It's Sheila's birthday in a fortnight, and we're having a party to celebrate.'

'What with?' asked Roger.

'Oh, we can always raise a fiver or so.'

'Well, you'd better raise eight fivers,' said Roger.

'That's a different thing altogether, old boy. Just can't be done.'

'Then you'll go to prison.'

'But I'll lose my job.'

'Haven't you any furniture you can sell?'

'All on hp, old boy. Only just started to pay for it.'

'Car?'

'Still in the Watford by-pass, I should think.'

'I thought you had it repaired?'

'That was the other fellow's.'

'Mr Thursby,' intervened Mr Trent, 'please don't think me impertinent, but are you quite sure about this particular judge?'

'Absolutely,' said Roger. 'I was down there last Thursday and he sent a chap to jail for six weeks because he'd been gambling. Only gave him seven days to pay.'

'Oh, well,' said Mr Trent, 'I'm afraid there's nothing for it.'

'Come, come,' said Mrs Starling, '*you're* not going to let us down, Fergie. Frank just can't go to jail. I won't have it, I tell you. I'll speak to the judge myself and explain.'

'I'm afraid that wouldn't do any good, Mrs Starling,' said Roger.

'That's not very complimentary,' said Mrs Starling. 'I once got a bookie to give me five to one when he was showing four to one on his board.'

'I told you she was class,' put in Mr Starling.

'I'm afraid judges aren't like bookies.'

'Apparently he'll skin me just the same,' said Mr Starling.

'No,' said the solicitor mournfully. 'I'm afraid there's nothing for it.'

'Well, we can try,' said Roger.

'Try what?' said the solicitor.

'See if I can persuade the judge to give more time.'

'D'you think you'll succeed?'

'Quite frankly – I don't, but one can never be sure till it's happened.'

'No,' said the solicitor even more gloomily. 'There's nothing for it. I shall have to lend you ten pounds. It goes against the grain, but I shall have to. I wouldn't do it for you, Frank, but I've always had a soft spot for Sheila. So there we are. Thank you very much all the same, Mr Thursby. Sorry we shan't have the pleasure of seeing you at the County Court.'

'I'm afraid I don't quite understand,' said Roger.

He was quite prepared for anyone to withdraw instructions from him at any time, but in the first place he couldn't think what he had done to merit it yet, and secondly the solicitor's attitude was quite friendly. He was completely out of his depth.

'No alternative,' said Mr Trent.

'But ten pounds isn't any good,' said Roger. 'He'll need forty pounds and possibly some costs as well.'

'We'll just have to go bankrupt.'

Roger thought for a moment.

'But,' he said rather tentatively, 'don't you have to owe fifty pounds in order to go bankrupt?'

'Quite so,' said Mr Trent. 'Our friend only owes forty pounds. Quite correct. It costs ten pounds to go bankrupt. I lend him ten pounds. He then owes fifty pounds and has the funds necessary to enable him to go bankrupt.'

'Anyway,' said Mr Starling, 'I could rustle up some other debts if you really want them. I didn't know they'd be a help.'

'Will you excuse me a moment?' said Roger.

He left the room and went hurriedly to Henry.

'Look, Henry. Can you tell me something in a hurry?'

He then stated what had happened.

'Well, is that all right?' he asked. 'Will it work? What happens about the judgment summons if he goes bankrupt?'

'Yes, that's quite OK,' said Henry. 'Once a receiving order in bankruptcy is made against a man that's the end of the judgment summons. Incidentally he does not need to owe £50. Anyone who's unable to pay his debts, whatever they are, can file his own bankruptcy petition. But he does need £10 to do it.'

'And anyone can avoid going to prison under a judgment summons by going bankrupt?'

'Quite correct,' said Henry.

'Then why doesn't everyone do that?'

'Several reasons. Some people can't raise the ten pounds to go bankrupt.'

'So that a man with ten pounds can avoid going to prison and a man without can't?'

'Right again. Then people who are in business on their own account, or have furniture or property of their own, don't want to go bankrupt as it means the end of their business and the selling up of their property.'

'But if you're in a job and haven't any property, there isn't any snag about it?'

'Not normally, unless you don't like the stigma of bankruptcy.'

'I'd prefer the stigma of bankruptcy to that of jail.'

'I quite agree,' said Henry. 'Of course quite a number of judgment debtors don't go bankrupt because they don't know that they can get out of their difficulties that way. But I gather your client does, now.'

Roger thanked Henry and went hurriedly back to his clients. 'I'm so sorry to have left you. I just went to make sure that there are no snags about Mr Trent's suggestion. I gather you've got a job, Mr Starling?'

'That's right. It's called a job, but between you and me, old boy, it's grossly underpaid.'

'And your furniture's all on hire purchase. Well, then, Mr Trent's idea seems an excellent one provided you don't mind the stigma of bankruptcy.'

'What's that?' said Mrs Starling.

'The stigma,' repeated Roger.

'Hold everything,' said Mrs Starling. 'Could we use your telephone?'

241

'Why, certainly,' said Roger, puzzled.

'What is it, old girl?' said Mr Starling.

' "The Stigma." It's running in the 3.30. We've just got time.'

'Good show,' said Mr Starling. 'Gosh – wouldn't we have been wild if we'd missed that? Could I use the phone, old boy? Won't be a jiffy. How much, old girl, d'you think? Half a quid each way?'

'Make it a quid, sweetheart,' said Mrs Starling. 'Then we'll have the doings to go to Lingfield.'

'OK,' said Mr Starling. 'Which way do I go?' Roger showed him, and came back to his room whilst Mr Starling was making his investment.

'That's two pounds you've put on, is it?' he asked Mrs Starling.

'Yes,' she said. 'Wish I could have made it a fiver. You don't have things like that happening every day. It's bound to win.'

'D'you know anything about the horse?'

'Anything about it?' said Mrs Starling. 'What more d'you want? With a name like that it couldn't lose.'

Suddenly Mr Starling dashed in, almost like Mr Grimes. 'Look, old girl,' he said, 'there's an apprentice called Thursby riding it. Dare we risk a fiver?'

'Gosh, yes,' said his wife.

'OK, old girl.'

And Mr Starling rushed back to the telephone.

'That's a bit of luck,' said Mrs Starling. 'You haven't a paper, I suppose?'

'I've a *Times*,' said Roger.

'Thanks awfully.'

She looked for the sporting page.

'It's in the twenty-to-one others. That'll mean one hundred and twenty-five pounds. How many runners are there? One, two, three, four – ' she went on counting up to seventeen.

'Gosh, I wonder if he ought to do it on the tote. Some of it anyway. They might pay a hundred to one. Would you excuse me?'

She rushed to the door and almost collided with her husband coming back.

'Did you do any on the tote?' she asked excitedly. 'It's in the twenty-to-one others.'

'Relax, old girl,' said Mr Starling. 'Three quid each way on the tote. Two at SP. OK?'

For answer, Mrs Starling kissed him.

'Oh, darling, I'm so happy. We'll celebrate tonight. Who'd have thought it? "The Stigma" with Thursby up.'

'And he gets a seven-pound allowance, old girl.'

'Can he get down to the weight?'

She took *The Times* and looked at the sporting page again.

'Yes – easily. It's in the bag.'

'Please forgive me, Mr Thursby. I don't suppose you understand this sort of thing. It means a great deal to us.'

'As far as I can see,' said Roger, feeling much older than twenty-one, 'you've just backed a horse and stand to lose ten pounds, a sum which you're about to borrow from Mr Trent in order to go bankrupt.'

'Old boy,' said Mr Starling, 'it does sound a trifle odd put that way, but Fergie understands. We put him on a good thing once. I say, old girl, you didn't happen to see if there's anything to double it with, did you? Quick, let's have a look.'

He took *The Times* from her, and started reading out the names of horses.

'My godfathers,' he shouted, 'excuse me. "Jolly Roger" in the 4.30. I'll see if I can get a half-quid each way double.

Forgive me, old boy, I saw the name on the brief. Won't be a jiffy.'

He rushed out of the door and nearly crashed into Mr Grimes, who was about to make a telephone call from the clerks' room.

'So sorry, old boy,' said Mr Starling. 'Terribly urgent.' And took the receiver away from him.

Mr Grimes said nothing. For once he could not think of anything to say. Mr Starling might be a solicitor for aught he knew.

'Hullo, hullo – ' said Mr Starling frantically. 'Is that Vulgans? This is Frank Starling – Boozer. Are they off for the 3.30 yet? Oh, they are – damn – oh, well, can I hold for the result? Thanks so much.' He turned to Mr Grimes.

'Damned shame, old man,' he said. 'They're off.'

'Dear, dear, dear,' said Mr Grimes.

'Well, we'll get the result first anyway,' went on Mr Starling. 'Then we can put half the winnings on the next, can't we, old boy? That's better really than a double. Make sure we have a fat win, anyway. Not much in your line I gather, old man?'

'Oh, well, my dear fellow,' said Mr Grimes, 'it keeps the telephone operator busy, if nothing else.'

'I'm terribly sorry, old boy – what's that, what? Who between? It's a photo finish. Who? But of course you can say. No – that's too ridiculous. Excuse me a moment, old man. Don't hang up.'

Mr Starling rushed back to the pupils' room.

'It's a photo finish,' he announced excitedly.

'Who between?' asked his wife.

'Wouldn't say.'

'But that's absurd. They'll always tell you if you ask them. Excuse me.'

'You ask them, old girl.'

Mr and Mrs Starling rushed out of the room to the telephone in time to hear the last of Mr Grimes' remarks to Alec.

'I don't know what we're coming to, I really don't.'

Meantime Roger looked at the solicitor whose expression had hardly changed and who sat still, looking mournful.

'Odd,' said Roger, 'very odd.'

'Not when you've known them as long as I have,' said Mr Trent. 'They'd gamble their souls away if anyone would lay the odds. I'll bet – now look what they've got me doing. Until I met Frank I didn't know one end of a racehorse from the other. And now I can even understand the sporting edition of the evening papers. I actually read the stop press – to see how much they've lost.'

At that moment the door burst open and Mr and Mrs Starling rushed into the room.

'We've won, we've won, we've won,' they shouted, and proceeded to dance together round the room.

' "The Stigma" with Thursby up,' they shouted. 'Good old "Stigma," good old Thursby. Here, where's that silly piece of blue paper?'

He picked up the judgment summons which had been in front of Roger and tore it into small pieces.

The solicitor appeared quite unmoved.

'I'm glad they've won, anyway,' Roger said to him. Mr and Mrs Starling were too occupied in making frenzied calculations on Roger's *Times* to be spoken to. 'Aren't you?' he added.

'If you'd seen this happen as often as I have,' said Mr Trent, 'you wouldn't move a muscle. They'll spend it all in a week and then we'll be back where we started. Still, it's saved me ten pounds for the moment. But only for the moment,' he added sadly.

Mr and Mrs Starling continued with their calculations for a little time and then started to make suggestions to Roger for every kind of celebration. After just over a quarter of an hour of this Mr Starling suddenly said: 'Ought to be able to get the tote prices now, old girl. Would you excuse me?' He went out to telephone again. Meanwhile, Roger started looking at the sporting page of *The Times*. He glanced idly at the information about the meeting. A few minutes later the door opened slowly and a very dejected Mr Starling walked in. As soon as his wife saw him, she knew.

'What's happened, sweetheart?' she said anxiously. 'Objection?'

'Yes, confound it,' said her husband. 'By the stewards. Upheld. Upheld, now I ask you.'

'That's extraordinary,' said Roger. 'D'you know, I've just happened to see that the senior steward's name is Perkins.'

'Don't see anything funny in that, old man,' said Mr Starling gloomily.

'Well,' said Mr Trent, 'I said it was only for the moment.' He looked at his watch.

'Now we've missed the Bankruptcy Court. Never mind, we can do that tomorrow.'

Sadly Mr and Mrs Starling and their solicitor left Roger. When they had gone, Roger said to Henry that he thought Judge Perkins must be quite a good judge.

CHAPTER TWENTY-FIVE

The End of the Beginning

By the time Roger had almost finished his pupillage he had certainly acquired a good deal of knowledge and experience and his confidence was correspondingly increased. He had earned the magnificent sum of sixty guineas. (It had, of course, cost his mother one hundred and ten guineas to enable him to do so.) He had opened his mouth sufficiently often in Court that he had long since ceased to hear his voice echoing above him. Although he still felt intensely nervous when left, or about to be left, by Mr Grimes to do part of a case in the High Court and although, as Henry had prophesied, he was still quite unfit to conduct a whole case there, he was in a very different condition from that in which he had started. He had learned a great deal from Mr Grimes and almost as much from Henry.

In a Magistrate's Court or a County Court he started to feel fairly comfortable and, although likely to be defeated there by more experienced advocates, he did not make nearly as many mistakes as most beginners make. He had taken Henry's and Charles' experiences to heart. A few days before his time was up Henry said to him: 'I'm sure that Grimeyboy will ask you to stay on here, if you want to. You're going to be very useful to him.'

'D'you really think so?'

'I've no doubt about it. There's another side to the question, though. How useful will he be to you? Well, you'll get a lot of experience and plenty of work. But unfortunately all his work is in the High Court and what you want is somewhere where there's plenty of smaller stuff about. Alec, no doubt, would do his best for you, but to get a County Court practice going in chambers where there isn't any small work is a pretty tough proposition. I think you'd do it in the end, but it'll be slow.'

'Then, what's your suggestion?'

'Well,' said Henry, 'something phenomenal has happened. I'm going to move.'

'You?'

'Yes. I've suddenly decided to try and do a bit more work. Sally's behind it, of course. I don't suppose it will last long. But she's persuaded me I ought to get out of this rut.'

'Where are you going?'

'Well, I know Mountview pretty well and his chambers are simply bursting with work. He said he'd like to have me there if I'd come. And I'm going.'

'I shall miss you,' said Roger. 'Can I come across and ask you anything when I want to?'

'You can come across altogether, if you want.'

'Move with you, d'you mean?'

'I do. I suppose you'll ask me what I advise. Well – ' began Henry.

'I'm not going to do anything of the sort. If that's a firm offer, I'll accept. I know a good thing when I see it, even at my stage.'

He thought for a moment.

'It is good of you,' he added. 'D'you think Grimeyboy will mind?'

'Grimeyboy never minds anything,' said Henry. 'He takes everything as it comes. He's always been the same and always will be. Dear, dear, dear. I don't know what things are coming to. They will do these things, my dear fellow, they will do these things.'

On the day on which his pupillage ended, Roger and Henry and Sally dined together. Roger was in high spirits.

'I don't know where I should be but for you two,' he said. 'Floating in the Thames, I should imagine, if I hadn't been picked up by now. D'you know I actually addressed the LCJ the other day?'

'What did you say?' asked Sally.

'Well,' said Roger, 'as a matter of fact it was – "if your Lordship pleases." '

'I hope he took it well,' said Henry.

'He said, "So be it," ' said Roger. 'I thought that was very decent of him. Now let's have a drink. And what shall we drink to? The future? Everyone's future, that is. I know what I want mine to be.'

'And I know mine,' said Henry.

'Me, too,' said Sally.

'I wonder,' said Roger, 'whether any of us will get what we want.'

'We shall see, my dear fellow, we shall see,' said Henry.

HENRY CECIL

ACCORDING TO THE EVIDENCE

Alec Morland is on trial for murder. He has tried to remedy the ineffectiveness of the law by taking matters into his own hands. Unfortunately for him, his alleged crime was not committed in immediate defence of others or of himself. In this fascinating murder trial you will not find out until the very end just how the law will interpret his actions. Will his defence be accepted or does a different fate await him?

THE ASKING PRICE

Ronald Holbrook is a fifty-seven-year-old bachelor who has lived in the same house for twenty years. Jane Doughty, the daughter of his next-door neighbours, is seventeen. She suddenly decides she is in love with Ronald and wants to marry him. Everyone is amused at first but then events take a disturbingly sinister turn and Ronald finds himself enmeshed in a potentially tragic situation.

'The secret of Mr Cecil's success lies in continuing to do superbly what everyone now knows he can do well.'
The Sunday Times

HENRY CECIL

BRIEF TALES FROM THE BENCH

What does it feel like to be a Judge? Read these stories and you can almost feel you are looking at proceedings from the lofty position of the Bench.

With a collection of eccentric and amusing characters, Henry Cecil brings to life the trials in a County Court and exposes the complex and often contradictory workings of the English legal system.

'Immensely readable. His stories rely above all on one quality – an extraordinary, an arresting, a really staggering ingenuity.'
New Statesman

HUNT THE SLIPPER

Harriet and Graham have been happily married for twenty years. One day Graham fails to return home and Harriet begins to realise she has been abandoned. This feeling is strengthened when she starts to receive monthly payments from an untraceable source. After five years on her own Harriet begins to see another man and divorces Graham on the grounds of his desertion. Then one evening Harriet returns home to find Graham sitting in a chair, casually reading a book. Her initial relief turns to anger and then to fear when she realises that if Graham's story is true, she may never trust his sanity again. This complex comedy thriller will grip your attention to the very last page.

HENRY CECIL

SOBER AS A JUDGE

Roger Thursby, the hero of *Brothers in Law* and *Friends at Court*, continues his career as a High Court judge. He presides over a series of unusual cases, including a professional debtor and an action about a consignment of oranges which turned to juice before delivery. There is a delightful succession of eccentric witnesses as the reader views proceedings from the Bench.

'The author's gift for brilliant characterisation makes this a book that will delight lawyers and laymen as much as did its predecessors.' *The Daily Telegraph*

THE WANTED MAN

When Norman Partridge moves to Little Bacon, a pretty country village, he proves to be a kind and helpful neighbour and is liked by everyone. Initially it didn't seem to matter that no one knew anything about his past or how he managed to live so comfortably without having to work.

Six months before, John Gladstone, a wealthy bank-robber had escaped from custody. Gradually, however, Partridge's neighbours begin to ask themselves questions. Was it mere coincidence that Norman Partridge had the build and features of the escaped convict? While some villagers are suspicious but reluctant to report their concerns to the police, others decide to take matters into their own hands...

OTHER TITLES BY HENRY CECIL AVAILABLE DIRECT
FROM HOUSE OF STRATUS

Quantity		£	$(US)	$(CAN)	€
☐	ACCORDING TO THE EVIDENCE	6.99	12.95	19.95	13.50
☐	ALIBI FOR A JUDGE	6.99	12.95	19.95	13.50
☐	THE ASKING PRICE	6.99	12.95	19.95	13.50
☐	BRIEF TALES FROM THE BENCH	6.99	12.95	19.95	13.50
☐	THE BUTTERCUP SPELL	6.99	12.95	19.95	13.50
☐	CROSS PURPOSES	6.99	12.95	19.95	13.50
☐	DAUGHTERS IN LAW	6.99	12.95	19.95	13.50
☐	FATHERS IN LAW	6.99	12.95	19.95	13.50
☐	FRIENDS AT COURT	6.99	12.95	19.95	13.50
☐	FULL CIRCLE	6.99	12.95	19.95	13.50
☐	HUNT THE SLIPPER	6.99	12.95	19.95	13.50
☐	INDEPENDENT WITNESS	6.99	12.95	19.95	13.50
☐	MUCH IN EVIDENCE	6.99	12.95	19.95	13.50

ALL HOUSE OF STRATUS BOOKS ARE AVAILABLE FROM GOOD BOOKSHOPS
OR DIRECT FROM THE PUBLISHER:

Internet: www.houseofstratus.com including synopses and features.

Email: sales@houseofstratus.com
info@houseofstratus.com
(please quote author, title and credit card details.)

OTHER TITLES BY HENRY CECIL AVAILABLE DIRECT
FROM HOUSE OF STRATUS

Quantity		£	$(US)	$(CAN)	€
	NATURAL CAUSES	6.99	12.95	19.95	13.50
	NO BAIL FOR THE JUDGE	6.99	12.95	19.95	13.50
	NO FEAR OR FAVOUR	6.99	12.95	19.95	13.50
	THE PAINSWICK LINE	6.99	12.95	19.95	13.50
	PORTRAIT OF A JUDGE	6.99	12.95	19.95	13.50
	SETTLED OUT OF COURT	6.99	12.95	19.95	13.50
	SOBER AS A JUDGE	6.99	12.95	19.95	13.50
	TELL YOU WHAT I'LL DO	6.99	12.95	19.95	13.50
	TRUTH WITH HER BOOTS ON	6.99	12.95	19.95	13.50
	UNLAWFUL OCCASIONS	6.99	12.95	19.95	13.50
	THE WANTED MAN	6.99	12.95	19.95	13.50
	WAYS AND MEANS	6.99	12.95	19.95	13.50
	A WOMAN NAMED ANNE	6.99	12.95	19.95	13.50

ALL HOUSE OF STRATUS BOOKS ARE AVAILABLE FROM GOOD BOOKSHOPS
OR DIRECT FROM THE PUBLISHER:

Tel: Order Line
         0800 169 1780 (UK)
          800 724 1100 (USA)
         International
         +44 (0) 1845 527700 (UK)
         +01   845 463 1100 (USA)

Fax: +44 (0) 1845 527711 (UK)
         +01   845 463 0018 (USA)
         (please quote author, title and credit card details.)

Send to: House of Stratus Sales Department   House of Stratus Inc.
          Thirsk Industrial Park   2 Neptune Road
          York Road, Thirsk   Poughkeepsie
          North Yorkshire, YO7 3BX   NY 12601
          UK   USA

PAYMENT

Please tick currency you wish to use:

☐ £ (Sterling)   ☐ $ (US)   ☐ $ (CAN)   ☐ € (Euros)

Allow for shipping costs charged per order plus an amount per book as set out in the tables below:

CURRENCY/DESTINATION

	£(Sterling)	$(US)	$(CAN)	€(Euros)
Cost per order				
UK	1.50	2.25	3.50	2.50
Europe	3.00	4.50	6.75	5.00
North America	3.00	3.50	5.25	5.00
Rest of World	3.00	4.50	6.75	5.00
Additional cost per book				
UK	0.50	0.75	1.15	0.85
Europe	1.00	1.50	2.25	1.70
North America	1.00	1.00	1.50	1.70
Rest of World	1.50	2.25	3.50	3.00

PLEASE SEND CHEQUE OR INTERNATIONAL MONEY ORDER
payable to: HOUSE OF STRATUS LTD or HOUSE OF STRATUS INC. or card payment as indicated

STERLING EXAMPLE

Cost of book(s):. . . . . Example: 3 x books at £6.99 each: £20.97
Cost of order: . . . . Example: £1.50 (Delivery to UK address)
Additional cost per book:. . . . . Example: 3 x £0.50: £1.50
Order total including shipping:. . . . . Example: £23.97

VISA, MASTERCARD, SWITCH, AMEX:

☐ ☐ ☐ ☐ ☐ ☐ ☐ ☐ ☐ ☐ ☐ ☐ ☐ ☐ ☐ ☐ ☐ ☐

Issue number (Switch only):

☐ ☐ ☐

Start Date: Expiry Date:

☐☐/☐☐   ☐☐/☐☐

Signature:

NAME:

ADDRESS:

COUNTRY:

ZIP/POSTCODE:

Please allow 28 days for delivery. Despatch normally within 48 hours.

Prices subject to change without notice.
Please tick box if you do not wish to receive any additional information. ☐

House of Stratus publishes many other titles in this genre; please check our website (**www.houseofstratus.com**) for more details.